THE SQUARE AND THE TRIANGLE

The Power of Integrating Relationships and Results in Workplace Culture

MARK STEVENS

Softcover ISBN: 978-1-61206-146-7
Hardcover ISBN: 978-1-61206-147-4
eBook ISBN: 978-1-61206-148-1

Interior and Cover Design by: Fusion Creative Works, FusionCW.com
Lead Editor: Jennifer Regner
Production Team: Aloha Publishing

For more information, visit TheSquareandtheTriangle.com.

To purchase this book at highly discounted prices, go to AlohaPublishing.com or email alohapublishing@gmail.com.

Published by

AlohaPublishing.com

Printed in the United States of America

This book is dedicated to two women. Both have instilled in me a love for language, leading, and life. To my mom, Barbara, who made the English language and a love of history worth pursuing. A child couldn't have asked for a better mentor. Thank you and loads of love. And to Shelly, my amazing and beautiful wife. She, more than anyone, has inspired me, helped to shape me, and opened my eyes to possibilities I didn't know existed—about being a friend, a spouse, a parent, and a leader.

Contents

Section I
Foundation

Keeping things simple makes action easier. When you can remember what you need to do under pressure, you'll be able to perform. If you keep leadership simple, success will follow.

Your job as a leader is to foster relationships and achieve results. Anything more adds complexity and doesn't serve you, your people, or your customers.

Balance is achieved when the foundation you build supports the weight you put on it. It's the same with leadership. Being aware of your natural ability to either build relationships or achieve results creates your foundation for integrating the other (Square or Triangle) and will help you do both better.

Section III
Putting It All Together

Your leadership success is rooted in how you manage the Square and the Triangle. By leading through your natural abilities, you can improve both how you build relationships and achieve results.

Leadership is rewarding. Getting better at leadership doesn't necessarily have to be difficult or painful. Personal accountability will come most naturally when you take the time to understand others, take the time to understand yourself, and find fun ways to approach growth.

"Occam's razor: a scientific and philosophical rule that entities should not be multiplied unnecessarily, which is interpreted as requiring that the simplest of competing theories be preferred to the more complex or that explanations of unknown phenomena be sought first in terms of known quantities."

—Merriam-Webster online dictionary

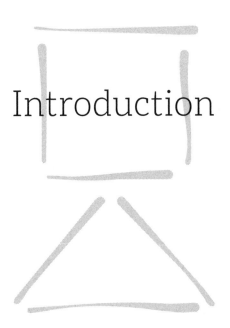

Introduction

"You can't fire a cannon off a bamboo platform."

—Mark Stevens

A few years ago, part of my personal "platform" for fitness and recreation was compromised by my knees. I'm an enthusiastic recreational cyclist. I once faced the unenviable decision of selling my bicycles because riding them caused knee pain I couldn't resolve on my own.

As a cyclist, my bike was more than just something to do. It was my path to freedom, to stress relief, to a world I couldn't find behind the windshield of a car. Sadly, my knee issue—iliotibial band pain or ITB pain to be precise—was going to end my cycling lifestyle in a quick but miserable exploration of online sales and bicycle reduction.

Fortunately, before I took that step, I decided to reach out for help. I found the Boulder Center for Sports Medicine. What made this find so incredible, beyond their therapeutic treatment and ultimate saving of my knee and my love of cycling, was something completely different—something that resonated beyond the bike.

The Boulder Center's motto was this: "If you're active, you're an athlete." Brilliant! All of us are athletes. *Really*. Because being active comes in many forms, and I'm betting all of us are active in some way.

They solved my knee pain because they had experience with my condition.

Through my work with leaders over the past 10 years, I've gained experience in solving all kinds of leadership problems and improving fundamental leadership skills. So now, let me help you solve your leadership dilemma (you may be wondering if you *have* a dilemma). You may not have a dilemma or may not realize yet that you have one, but every organization benefits from improved leadership abilities.

It's this simple: If you influence people, you're a leader. And like many people, you've probably had those moments when you just couldn't find it within you to lead better. Whether it was on the job or at home, you couldn't find a way to connect better with those around you and get things accomplished. You're reading this book because you're ready to get better.

And you should be reading *this* book because of the thousands of leadership books available, this book will show you a path to improvement that is so simple in concept, you can put it to work right away. No complex formulas, graphs, reports, or mile-long lists of leadership adjectives.

With this book, you'll get a simple, tested way to understand and improve your leadership and enjoy—and sustain—the relationships and results you crave.

I worked for a period of time with a company that had a pretty good handle on leadership. During that time, I helped develop a small team that was laser-focused on how to help the staff function better. The company had the requisite library of leadership skills and competencies so common with bigger organizations. Armed with these skills, it should have been as simple as helping these leaders focus their work around those skills, learn how to apply them, and then conquer the world.

What I found was that while the skills themselves made sense, the team seemed to lack the understanding of how to apply them. There were too many skills and so many ways to define leadership—so many complicating twists—that these leaders were clueless as to where to start improving their leadership.

This came to a head one Saturday as we all met in a conference room at the site, pondering how our committee was going to advance the performance of the staff and drive leadership development forward. We discussed the company's competencies in gory detail but still, there wasn't a simple way to easily apply them and understand how to improve performance. I remember trying to help my peers understand how we were overcomplicating the complicated. It didn't need to be this hard.

"But we have to be accountable. And *hold* people accountable!" one cried.

"And we have to communicate!" said another.

"And think . . . critically!"

"What about results?"

"And planning!"

"And being courageous!"

They reminded me of many other adjectives, too. It was pretty defeating after a while.

And that's when it hit me.

"Guys, at the end of the day, we need people to get things done, right?" I asked.

"Yes," came the answer.

I said, "Let me tell you a story from my days in martial arts."

The story goes like this. It's simple, phenomenally simple. My instructor told the class one night what he had been taught: "You can't fire a cannon off a bamboo platform." The idea was pretty intuitive. If you don't have a good base under you, you won't be able to throw a punch or a kick, or block something coming your way. Moreover, that base needed to be flexible so it could move and adjust. A cannon on top of bamboo isn't going to stay there very long. Even less time when you fire it.

How about on concrete? Better. Concrete won't fall apart when you fire the cannon.

But what about a mobile base, with lockable wheels? You can point it and shoot it and move it. Even better!

I told my friends at the site this story. I even jumped up and struck a pose—a flashy stance with a punch ready to go. At first, they kind of laughed at me and asked me what I was talking about. I told them this: "You need a good foundation to leverage what you're going to deliver. If the base is strong, it will tolerate the weight of what you put on it."

Nods in the room. Okay, makes sense. Go on . . .

I told them that leadership is about the base. If you have a good foundation, you can put weight on it. See?

Uh, kinda . . .

I drew a cannon on the whiteboard. And then a square base under it . . .

And then it struck me.

"Guys, see the block under the cannon?" Nods. "Let's imagine that the base is this square," I continued. "See how *solid* it appears? Now let's imagine it looks like this." I drew a triangle under the square. "Assume this square is the cannon on top of the triangle. See how unstable that looks?"

My buddies looked at it closely. And one, in particular, really latched on.

"I get it!" he exclaimed. "I can see the instability. Tell me, what is that square? And what is the triangle?"

It took a few minutes to flesh out, with the ideas coming rapidly. But within a few minutes it was there on the white board for all to see: a hastily drawn square and a ragged triangle.

I said, "This square is all about relationships. It's the *people* part of leadership. How we talk to them, connect with them, earn their trust. And this triangle is about getting work done. It's about results and drive and pushing the team."

They stared. They wondered. They asked me for more.

"See how they connect?" I put the triangle over the square. It looked like a little house. "See? The foundation is right there—

that square is the platform—better than bamboo. And that triangle is the cannon. Now compare."

I erased the board, complete with cannons, squares, and triangles, and drew two simple constructs: a square under a triangle and a triangle under a square. "See the difference?" I asked.

"Yes, but what does it mean?" my friend asked.

I told them that not all people are naturally good at relationships. I pointed to one of our partners in the room. "Guys, Joe over there is all about the people. He's the square on the bottom. But Steve? You know him. That guy is all about results. His *base* is that triangle. And if he's not careful, that square will fall right off!"

They nodded again. "You see, everyone needs both this square and this triangle. We need our people and we need to get results. Simple. But each of us approaches our work and our leadership from one strength or the other. This might seem oversimplified, but it's really that easy. The 'people' people need to leverage their foundation, their strength, in relationships to get the work done. That's their base—their platform. And the 'results' people need to leverage their *get-it-done* style along with making sure they don't lose their audience. That triangle is their base, their strength."

They were catching on.

"See, you all have a foundational type and if you know it, you can learn to balance the other on top. So, it doesn't matter if you're a square at the bottom or a triangle. As long as you know who you are. And then you can focus your leadership development on these two things—not 12 or 15 or 50. See?"

This conversation was the origin of the Square and the Triangle approach to understanding leadership. It led to more discussions, which led to further refinement over time—including the importance of realizing you require both types of skills to be an effective leader. But it was this pivotal conversation that brought the concept to life and led me down a fascinating and rewarding path that has made leadership a reality for so many. Now, I've had the good fortune to witness 10 years' worth of Squares and Triangles and to watch leaders' eyes open wide and their minds open wider. Now, it's your turn.

I want to note that we all lead in many aspects of our lives. It's not just in business circles. While the main audience for this book is people leading in business, these concepts can apply in many parts of your life: family, church, sports, school. There really are no limits. These concepts can not only enrich your work, they can enrich your life, which also has the benefit of providing you ample places to practice. So be creative and open as you look for opportunities to apply these ideas.

If you influence people, you're a leader. Let me help you get there faster and easier than you ever dreamed possible.

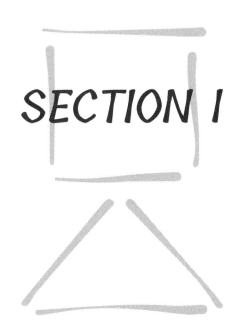

SECTION I

Foundation

1

Why Simplicity?

Keeping things simple makes action easier. When you can remember what you need to do under pressure, you'll be able to perform. If you keep leadership simple, success will follow.

William of Ockham was a Franciscan philosopher and theologian in the fourteenth century. His philosophy of explaining how one might ponder complex problems became known as Occam's razor. While it might be too simple even for William of Ockham, his theory often gets restated to something like this: when faced with competing solutions or ideas, the simple one is likely the right one.

I don't know what William of Ockham knew about leadership, but I do think he was on to something, math and science aside. Simple solutions are often the right solutions.

Let me give you an example. Your peer at work fails to say hello to you one day. You could try to guess why:

1. He is having a bad day and just isn't in the mood for conversation.

2. It's possible she just doesn't like you anymore because of some indiscretion you're not aware of, but you're certain it wasn't your fault.

3. While driving to work, he was shaken by seeing a terrible accident that he just can't get off his mind and isn't really "there" when you walk by.

4. She just didn't see you—regardless of why.

Some of these possibilities imply feelings or motivations that could make working together difficult, but they may not be real. Unless you ask, you won't know.

We tell ourselves stories all the time about the events in our lives. Complex stories—because we have a need for things to be rich in detail because we're rich and complex people. It's rewarding to know that our lives demand a tapestry of detail to appeal to the unique qualities we see in ourselves, and complexity equals worth.

But is that really true? Or necessary?

Let's look at this from the position of complexity. Aside from confirming with your peer what actually caused her not to say hello, is it possible the situation was more complex than just not seeing you? Of course. However, what is to be gained from making it complex? Creating an unconfirmed story may have prevented you from making the simple decision to ask how she was doing.

Creating complexity, or assuming complexity, creates a lot more work for you in any situation. Without exploring the situation first, you immediately put yourself in the situation of having to sort out your assumptions from the facts. Assuming complexity is slower than starting simply and branching out.

If you look at the history of medicine, think of the simple solutions that have saved lives and made healthcare better. Here's one everyone can do: wash your hands. The Centers for Disease Control and Prevention have worked hard to make sure we all know and understand why handwashing is so important. It removes germs that can make us and others sick. Simple. Healthcare isn't always this easy but the point is clear. Good health doesn't have to solely rely on complex solutions that are hard to teach or understand. When faced with the complexity of germs, the solution was simple. Wash them off.

Ben Carlson, chartered financial analyst, describes why "simple" works in finance through his blog *A Wealth of Common Sense*. He describes that complexity can lead to unanticipated consequences, and it can give you the illusion of control (not actually *being* in control). Further, he supports the idea that complex problems don't require complex solutions.

If complex concepts like medicine and personal finance can be addressed through simple solutions, why can't leadership?

Life need not be complicated to be rich in its rewards. Why can't flowers just be beautiful? Why can't a hug just feel good? Yes, there is science to all that and likely some theories we still don't entirely understand, but why must the simplest things in life be so overcomplicated?

Holding hands just feels right. Do it more.

Sunshine on your face feels good. Go outside.

And leadership doesn't have to involve a 15-point plan with a myriad of check-ins and forms and technology to work. I'm telling you, it doesn't have to be this hard.

SIMPLICITY AND PRESSURE

I'm no different than many people. Likely, no different than you. I wanted to be better at leading people. I went looking for ways to get better and I found them. Lots of them. But I noticed that almost all of those ways were consistently complex. From colored wheels to chemistry-esque formulas, there were so many rich and varied approaches to leading that I was becoming quite confident that I'd never really get better. I mean, how could I remember all that, let alone put it into practice?

It won't take long, if you go to the bookstore or do some research online, to identify literally hundreds of "competencies" or "skills" that define what and how a leader should be. Some resonated with me and some didn't. But in the end, even with casting aside the duplicates and the imponderables, I was still left with a staggering number of adjectives I would have to figure out how to apply.

It was really too much to think about.

Especially under pressure.

I referred to my martial arts training when I told the story of the cannon and the bamboo platform. Let me share another learning: It has been said that the "black belt" of martial art fame was nothing more than a sash the practitioner wore in ancient times. It just wouldn't do to have a local starving hero wandering around with a cloak that continued to fall open. It has also been said that the sash, which started out white, would become dirty and soiled over time. Let's face it, martial arts heroes weren't changing out their belts with popular colors to display their prowess and technique. How would anyone really know what a "green belt" meant or a "purple belt" signified?

The belt just got darker and darker with time and use. Those with darker, (i.e., blacker) belts would be more experienced. Occam's razor in practice. Such a simple explanation.

Now, more to the point. It has also been said that the definition of a "black belt" is a person who, under pressure, can remember three techniques *correctly*. As a martial artist, I learned hundreds of techniques, but under pressure—more plainly, a 250-pound enemy chasing me down, ready to pummel me—I might only be able to manage one or two things correctly. Performing a martial art technique badly means not only having little effect on the other person, it could mean personal injury. Try punching anything remotely hard, if you haven't trained for it. Can you say broken hand?

If, under pressure, I could only accomplish one or two or three things correctly, I had to ask myself: Why was I practicing so many techniques? Why not practice one or two and get them down pat? Hmmm.

While most things aren't quite that simple, it really isn't far from the truth. In my martial arts class, we all had our "signature" move—the one thing we could count on. We all practiced it. A lot. It's not that all those other moves and techniques didn't serve a purpose. They absolutely did. But building those elements around something that could be relied upon under pressure made a big difference. And it simplified the training in many respects.

Leadership is fundamentally no different. If you practice something a lot, you'll more than likely be able to rely on it under pressure.

SIMPLICITY AND FOCUS

So, with hundreds of leadership principles to practice, where do you start?

What if I were to tell you there were *only two?*

If there were only two competencies, it would make the process of practice that much easier. And if there were only two, you could more quickly identify what your true talent is—and isn't.

Leadership doesn't have to be complex to be effective.

In fact, I would argue that if leadership is too complex, it's hard to be effective—for yourself and for others. But simplifying leadership doesn't have to mean dumbing it down or being so limited that it lacks nuance. Beauty and depth can come from the simplest expressions. Just look at a Chinese watercolor painting and you'll see what I mean.

William of Ockham wasn't suggesting that simple means a lack of depth. William suggested that if you're looking at a problem, and lots of ideas and possible solutions present themselves, the simplest one is often the right one. So, while I'm suggesting that there are really only two things you need to focus on, those two things independently and collectively have a lot of depth. You can spend a lifetime perfecting them.

What's appealing in all of this is that having two areas to focus on quickly moves your mind from wondering where to start to actually doing something to improve.

The Square and the Triangle, as you'll see, are perfect partners in your drive for a simple approach to becoming a better leader. They have the advantage of helping you focus on your area of strength and where you need to improve, while encompassing enough depth to make the journey not only interestingly introspective but ultimately effective and rewarding.

Having a simple approach to leadership will focus your efforts more acutely on those aspects you want to develop and build upon. If your weak areas are in the Triangle, you can quickly realize that and get to work. You don't need to spend hours attempting to parse out just the right competency to improve. Because, as you'll discover, the relationship between the Square and the Triangle helps to shine a light on the aspects you need to work on.

The same can be said of strengths. If your general leadership tendencies fall within the Square, then you should take the time to understand why and what it can do for you. It's the classic phrase, "Go with what you know." By being able to quickly pin down what your strong suit is, you can make quicker work of learning how to leverage what you do well.

This might sound almost unbelievably easy—maybe too much so. But I've spent years watching leaders, who invested a lot of time in much more complicated models, have that fore-head-slapping moment when they realized they'd been spending too much time on researching leadership and not enough time practicing it. Complexity is ultimately what stood in the way. Once the lesson became understandable, they got focused, encouraged, and far more resilient in finding ways to balance their Square or Triangle strengths than trying to determine what competency breakdown was at the root of their suffering.

SIMPLICITY AND UNDERSTANDING

So, simplicity makes performing under pressure easier and helps you focus on what to work on.

Simplicity also makes leadership easier to grasp, for you and those around you. Leadership development programs tend to be rooted in feedback, as they should be. You probably have formed an opinion of yourself, and it's probably a pretty good one. The issue is that just as often, others may see you differently than you see yourself. It's a real conundrum. You want to believe you're a solid leader, but when your peers get asked, they tend to tell a different story. It may not be all bad, mind you, but their version doesn't always compare equally to your own.

At an organization I worked for, we polled a group of leaders to gauge their perceptions. This was done at a pretty high level—senior management. It was a sizeable group, a big company with a few hundred leaders. They were asked a few questions—namely, how did they perceive their own leadership? And how did they perceive the leadership of others? How did they themselves live up to the company's values? And how did they believe their peers did so?

The results were quite interesting. As you can imagine, when people talked about themselves, the majority felt they were all quite talented at leadership. But when they discussed others, they found the group lacking in ability. When discussing values, the team saw themselves as true stewards of company values. However, when focused on their peers, the team found them not as value-driven as they saw themselves.

So, here we were in a room of many self-proclaimed great leaders, working with a bunch of so-so leaders and values ambassadors.

That's the value of feedback. It was an eye-opening moment for the team to realize the collective belief in the group was that we had work to do. Had people relied solely on their own opinions of themselves, they might have lacked the impetus to improve.

Simplicity is important in this aspect. If someone is going to give me feedback, it's important they understand what they are describing to me. By way of example, I highly recommend you don't ask me to check your calculus homework. I can give you feedback but it will come with a strong disclaimer that you shouldn't take a test based on what I tell you. However, when I know what I'm talking about and you know what I'm describing, that feedback can be more value-added for both of us.

The Square and the Triangle are surprisingly useful this way. What has been the most impressive to me is that the groups I've taught were literally able to use the Square and the Triangle terms as a "language" for feedback. They were able to clearly see where they believed they were strong and where they felt they had room to grow. While I taught them the concepts, the language development aspect was an organic benefit I didn't see coming. It made me all the more confident that I was onto something that could drive learning and growth in others.

By taking a simple approach, my students were able to immediately relate to each other and help direct one another down a path to better leadership. Leadership development isn't a solo path. You can do parts of it on your own and hope to succeed—and maybe you will succeed—but ultimately, your growth comes from the feedback others give you. Keeping the learning easy to digest but delicious enough to savor has been one of the most important benefits from the Square and the Triangle approach.

While feedback is important, its main purpose is to address the concept of self-awareness. If, as a leader, you're having difficulty assessing yourself—your strengths and weaknesses—feedback can help direct you. However, you must ultimately develop the ability to assess yourself through self-awareness. As a leader, you need both the Square and the Triangle. You aren't just one or the other. It will become obvious over time that you tend to lean toward one, but you require both types of skills to be an effective leader. Self-awareness, augmented by feedback, will be one of the most important tools you'll need in order to adapt your leadership style and find the right balance between the Square and the Triangle.

TAKE-HOME MESSAGES

△ Simple solutions are often the right solutions.

△ Keeping things simple keeps you focused.

△ Simplicity keeps you nimble under pressure.

2

Relationships and Results

Your job as a leader is to foster relationships and achieve results. Anything more adds complexity and doesn't serve you, your people, or your customers.

WHY ONLY TWO COMPETENCIES?

I'm hoping I have convinced you that simple really can be better. I'm confident that taking a simpler approach to developing your leadership will yield greater results and less frustration than a more complicated one. With this in mind, why two competencies and not three? Why not one?

There is a limit to how far something can be narrowed down for the sake of simplicity. Think about how you communicate with your doctor about your health, for example. Going to the doctor and saying your body hurts is a bit too vague for the physician to give personalized and useful advice. Indicating that you have a headache will give the doctor a much better shot at getting the answers he or she needs to help you. The same is true in learning about the way you lead: just getting the feedback that your leadership needs improvement, without any specifics, is probably not helpful.

The value of working with two competencies is that it's focused and easy to grasp. However, each of those two areas has significant depth. I've worked with hundreds of leaders and in every case, those leaders all had to accomplish two things: they had to lead people and they had a job to do. It isn't more complex than that. However, by giving specific feedback on those two areas, I could provide sufficient detail about how a leader might approach improving his or her performance.

The key behind the two areas, *relationships* (the Square) and *results* (the Triangle), is the depth beneath the surface of each idea. That depth inspires more detailed and yet surprisingly simple feedback. By starting broadly but not too broad, I could help leaders focus their thinking where it belonged. In the past, when I relied on hyper-specific competency models, my feedback got too detailed too quickly, and it almost always resulted in less clarity up front and the need for more conversation about what I was really trying to say.

If you go to the doctor, the physician is likely going to begin investigating broadly and work inward. If he starts with the headache, he can work from what that might mean—is it in the front of the head or the back? Does the pain radiate or stay constant? Any vision issues, etc.?

What the doctor isn't likely to do is tell you, without digging deep, that you have Peruvian sheep milk allergies, which are creating headaches in your frontal lobe, and then ask if that sounds reasonable to you. Okay, I'm being facetious—but the point is clear. Starting with a broad approach and then working toward a more detailed analysis can help pinpoint the pain. It's no different with leadership.

I've worked with leaders who were exposed to leadership models that included 15 or more competencies (I personally own a book that lists 119!) and when they gave feedback, they tended to diagnose right to the specific competency. They might tell their peer that he or she was suffering from an inability to communicate because in the company's competency list, "effective communication" was one of the competencies. The peer would invariably ask why that was the case, and the back and forth would begin.

Often, the competencies weren't truly understood. The peer's poor performance might have nothing to do with communication at all. Because of the organization's competency model, delivering hyper-specific feedback could easily occur. Invariably, this need to be hyper-specific meant a lot of hairsplitting by both leaders and peers, who might not be properly describing the real leadership issue at hand.

I've seen mentors criticize leaders (their mentees) for their communication foibles and tell them to go fix them. The risk was that the mentors, in looking at the organization's competency library, might focus too hard on what *competency* wasn't being properly performed instead of working with the leader first to understand more generally what issue was plaguing the leader. It was a case of looking up diagnoses without first doing an examination to determine the symptoms.

Does this mean organizations shouldn't have 15 competencies? Not at all. But they need to be understood in a context beyond the competencies themselves. The *interconnectivity* between the competencies is important.

Some organizations attempt to solve this by aligning their competencies in groupings like "People Leadership" or "Results Orientation." Is this the same as the Square and the Triangle? No, it's not. Those groupings are designed to drive you to specific details designed in the library they support and, in my experience, the groupings get forgotten. With the groupings forgotten, leaders again get trapped by the complexity of so many competencies.

By way of example, let me pick on the effective communication competency again. That competency often gets lumped in with "people leadership" or something similar. This is understandably so. People communicate with each other. They talk to each other. They write to one another. They look at each other—think nonverbal communication. It's easy to see how this gets categorized under a people leadership competency.

But communication is about more than just the *act* of communicating. It's about purpose, it's about desired outcomes, it's about manner and method. Communication is every bit as much about **results** as it is about **relationships.** So why *limit* the competency to people leadership?

Why not start more broadly, as the Square and the Triangle allow us to do, and then peel the onion back to see what's there? Communication is a skill for both the Square and the Triangle spaces. By using only two competencies and recognizing their broad but still definable spaces, leaders can more easily evaluate their own and others' performance and then do something about it.

Large-number competency models hope to accomplish this type of evaluation by being very specific and inclusive. While that may appear to create a large vocabulary for leaders to learn and play with, in the experiences of the leaders I've taught, it can be too much to digest and to practice. By eliminating the specificity associated with complex models, what I've found—and what the leaders I've supported have echoed—is that when using the simple Square and Triangle language they could more easily speak to leadership in a way that was manageable and understandable. The organic nature of the dialogue, and the directions it took them, helped leaders explore their own style and abilities without being needlessly burdened by a vocabulary that can't be everything but tries to be.

Let me put this another way: all you need is two.

FEELING VERSUS THINKING

I was very fortunate to practice HR in the healthcare arena and in multiple settings within that arena. Blood banking, home health, hospitals, and clinics. I was around a lot of patients and patient care providers. I also spent lots of time with all of the nonclinical staff (like me) who played a role in delivering care to the patient, albeit indirectly. What I learned very quickly was that patients, generally speaking, didn't spend a lot of time *thinking* about their care. From our routine and occasionally brilliant success stories to the thankfully rare tragic outcomes, patients and their families tended to *feel* about their care and their experiences rather than be intellectual about it. They loved the nurse who was so kind, they adored the physician who took time to explain things. Patients described their experiences in feelings as in "I felt heard" or "I felt cared for."

It was uncommon to receive an intellectual and technical vote of confidence. We didn't get letters that talked about the phlebotomist's technique or the accurate way the radiologist read the scan. People just don't talk that way.

They also had no problem telling us how they felt when they didn't have a good experience. They would tell us when they didn't feel heard; when they didn't feel we'd cared for them. Angry responses were never really rooted in the technical aspects of the care. Often, patients didn't know enough about medicine to know if things were done well or poorly, but they sure *felt* like it was good or bad, regardless of the facts.

Okay, that's how it was for healthcare. Makes sense. Life and death. But I saw it in everyday business too. I worked in my early career as a paint department manager for a major retailer. I learned a lot about paint while doing that job (including that I don't like painting). Here is a quick education about paint. Paint is made of up three things: rock, water, and glue. Rock is the pigment—the color of the paint. Water keeps the rock-particle mixture thin enough to apply, and the glue lets it stick to the wall. It's that simple (William of Ockham would be proud).

So, here's the deal. If the color of the paint was wrong, it came down to a few factors. The customer didn't have a good match from home or the paint wasn't mixed right (pigment is added to a bland base which yields the final color). And so on. Customers don't want paint colors to be wrong—and do you want to talk about *feelings*? When paint was the wrong color, customers didn't talk about rock, pigments, or paint-machine formulas. Nope. They just got red in the face (no pun intended by using a color metaphor) and told me how upset they were when the "ocean green" they wanted was replaced by "sea green." Yes, there's a difference. I wish the people naming the paint swatches used names that were more distinct and differentiated.

While I got a few complaints about colors being wrong, by far the most complaints were about the paint not sticking—in particular, to the outside of a house, i.e., exterior paint. To effectively paint the outside of a house (quick tip: have someone else do it for you), you need to be sure the house is truly and appropriately *prepped*. We routinely told folks the house has to be clean . . . I mean **clean** and **dry**. A favorite suggestion was to pressure-wash the house. Soon, all the dirt would be gone. And then people would paint the house.

Let me share the two most common paint complaints that weren't the fault of the paint, despite what we heard. It would go like this:

"This paint is defective," says the angry customer.

"Do you have a sample?" I would ask.

"Yes. Have a look." And a peeled piece of paint would be handed to me.

Invariably, I would see one of two scenarios. One: a paint chip with mounds of dirt on the back. The paint wasn't defective. It stuck just fine (remember the glue component). It had stuck to the *dirt* the painter hadn't washed off the house, rather than sticking to the house. Two: a peeled piece of paint with wood stuck to the back. The house hadn't been allowed to dry long enough after pressure washing. The painter would get too eager to finish before the weekend and paint too soon. The paint would dry and the siding couldn't *breathe,* causing the water to work inwards and the siding to rot and peel—taking the paint with it.

If you take my earlier remarks about patients and families to heart, the same could be said about paint. When something didn't seem right about their paint, people were angry. The facts weren't the issue. It was the disappointment at the mess, the expense of potentially replacing the paint, the feeling that some-one let them down. I'm not blaming painters or patients. I'm making the point that our feelings tend to drive our outlook on things, not the cold, hard details.

In my experience, leadership is no different. The Square and the Triangle help leaders *feel* their way through leadership as much as *think* about leadership. When the conversation can take an organic approach—and not be overly constrained by complex details and labels that fail to resonate—leadership be-comes more of a human condition that we can relate to instead of a set of sterile competencies we can't.

The Square and the Triangle allow the conversation to breathe. They allow a level of introspection that can be manage-able—even appealing to engage in—because you can feel your way through a leadership dialogue. For the leaders I've worked with, I'm always amazed at their emotional reaction to learning about the Square and the Triangle. That look in their eye, the way they just "get it" isn't an intellectual response, it's an emotional one. It almost borders on relief. This connection with the heart of leadership comes from a response to the pictures, not complex labels or systems. The geometric shapes (the Square and the Triangle) are used in place of those ideas. There is a kind of a code-breaking response in people—they can finally see and feel what they've been fighting to understand, sometimes for years. This is the beauty of the Square and the Triangle.

I've said repeatedly to managers I've worked with that I could teach this on the back of a napkin. That's a bit of a stretch but not by much. In this case, my experience shows that a picture is easily worth a thousand words. The nuance, and there is nuance, comes with repetition and digging deeply, but it's the picture that pulls people in. And when they truly *feel* they can become better leaders, when they honestly believe they have it in them, then they are well on their way to getting there. When a leader's development comes from an engaging sense of wonder and revelation—as opposed to an intellectual notion about improvement—he or she is more inclined to take the journey toward self-improvement.

WHY RELATIONSHIPS AND RESULTS?

So far, I've spent a lot of time throwing around the terms *relationships* and *results*, otherwise known as the Square and the Triangle. But why these two competencies? Why not "accountability" and "urgency" or "communication" and "transformation"? It's a fair question.

When I was meeting with the performance group I mentioned in the introduction, what we found was that certain issues plagued leaders more than others. Those leaders were asking themselves the same questions I've seen echoed hundreds of times over. "How do I get my people to perform?" "How do I deal with problem employees?" "How do I get my people to follow me?"

I've found that in every industry I've supported, these questions came up way more often than any other. As an HR professional, I have guided leaders on better hiring, policy interpretation, benefits, legal questions, etc., but the questions about helping people perform, especially about those who fail to perform, dominated my time. I learned to love employee relations issues because when leaders could help their teams perform better, the other leadership problems were easier to tolerate. Leaders certainly faced other challenging issues, from budget to safety to project management, but when staff failed to perform, it became nearly impossible for them to solve these other issues with any real success.

Dealing with poor performers robs leaders of the time they need to lead in other areas.

Performance issues often resulted from a disconnection between staff and the leaders. Staff weren't following directions. They didn't seem to be on the same track as their manager. This was true regardless of the level of the organization. I watched the senior-most leaders struggle with this and I watched line-level supervisors be equally flummoxed. Something was getting in the way of the connection between leaders and subordinates. Additionally, what resulted was that outcomes weren't matching the work of the team. They seemed to toil endlessly in an attempt to accomplish things, but they were either the wrong accomplishments or failed attempts at the right work.

Through constant diagnosis, which came about through thousands of hours of sitting down with leaders and staff, it became clearer and clearer to me, year after year, that how leaders and staff *related* to one another was impacting whether or not they were successful. I've heard it over and over again. "My manager doesn't speak to me." "My boss doesn't seem to understand me." "My boss doesn't care about me." Staff, which includes all of us—for the most part we all report to someone— want a relationship with their boss and they want their boss to be someone they can respect and count on.

The biggest problem in the relationship game is not to have one at all. The second biggest problem is to have a bad one.

There is a bit of a cause and effect here: good relationships create good results—and good relationships require work; a good relationship requires effort to create and maintain. When relationships don't work, things don't get done—i.e., no results. Results come from effort. When that effort doesn't come with good practice and direction, you're leaving the outcomes to chance.

The workplace need not be a place of toleration. You shouldn't have to just "get by" at work. When you care about what you do and you care about those you do it with, your work can be rewarding, rather than being just that part of the day that pays the bills. When relationships are built and leveraged appropriately, it's a lot easier to drive results.

I've had thousands of interactions with staff and leaders over my career. They all want the same thing; I'm comfortable saying that it's universal. Leaders and their teams want to care about the work they do and they want to be cared for by the workplace. *Relationships* and *results* drive the workplace, and it's why I've focused on them above any other definitions of leadership.

You might argue that leadership is more than these two things. However, if the complicated, multi-competency paths to leadership development and growth were the true bread and butter of building highly competent leaders, we'd have the answer already. If you accept that relationships and results are all you truly need to know and understand, then you can have the success the leaders I've worked with are having. I'm not saying it's easy just because it's simple. However, keeping your focus on these two items, and more importantly how they *balance* one another, will allow you to make gains in your leadership abilities much faster than if you get stuck in the complex competency rut that robs you of the energy to learn, grow, and prosper.

TAKE-HOME MESSAGES

△ Two competencies are easier to remember and use.

△ Leading is about thoughts *and* feelings.

△ Leading is about influencing people to achieve results.

Balance is achieved when the foundation you build supports the weight you put on it. It's the same with leadership. Being aware of your natural ability to either build relationships or achieve results creates your foundation for integrating the other (Square or Triangle) and will help you do both better.

WHAT DOES *BALANCE* MEAN?

Leadership development doesn't have to be complex. It really doesn't. When you let the power of simplicity clear your mind, you can see the path toward it right now and begin to make immediate strides forward.

The concept of *balance* is central to the Square and the Triangle. To be a leader, you must have both relationships and results. You can't have just one or the other. The key to these principles is how they balance each other. I want to make sure you understand what balance means in this context.

As a kid, I grew up with a mom who instilled in me a love for the English language. She loved words, she loved reading, and she loved the dictionary. She expected us kids (at least she seemed to expect me) to use words well and to understand them. So, when we failed to use a word correctly or even know what one meant, we were dispatched away to retrieve the dictionary and look it up. I recall having to come back and explain what I'd learned. I'm not sure she'd fully agree with this memory, as we all know what youth does to it, but I'm sticking with this story.

My research in *Merriam-Webster's Dictionary* online came up with no less than nine different definitions of balance.

DEFINITION OF BALANCE

1. an instrument for weighing: such as

    a) a beam that is supported freely in the center and has two pans of equal weight suspended from its ends

    b) a device that uses the elasticity of a spiral spring for measuring weight or force

2. a means of judging or deciding
    - the *balance* of a free election

3. a counterbalancing weight, force, or influence The comedic character serves as a *balance* to the serious subject matter of the play.

4. an oscillating wheel operating with a hairspring to regulate the movement of a timepiece

- a watch's *balance*

5. a) stability produced by even distribution of weight on each side of the vertical axis when the two sides of the scale are in *balance* tipped the statue off balance

b) equipoise between contrasting, opposing, or interacting elements

- . . . the *balance* we strike between security and freedom.

—Earl Warren

- Both parties were interviewed to provide *balance* in the report.

- the right *balance* of diet and exercise

c) *accounting*: equality between the totals of the two sides of an account

6. a) an aesthetically pleasing integration of elements achieving *balance* in a work of art

b) *grammar*: the juxtaposition in writing of syntactically parallel constructions containing similar or contrasting ideas (such as "to err is human; to forgive, divine")

7. a) physical equilibrium

- trouble keeping your balance on a sailboat

- lost his *balance* and fell

- a boxer kept off *balance* for a whole round

b) the ability to retain one's balance

- Gymnasts must have a good sense of *balance*.

8. **a)** weight or force of one side in excess of another • The *balance* of the evidence lay on the side of the defendant.

   b) something left over: remainder

   • answers will be given in the *balance* of this chapter.

   —R. W. Murray

   c) *accounting*: an amount in excess especially on the credit side of an account

   • has a comfortable balance in the bank

   • You must maintain a minimum *balance* of $1,000 in your account to avoid fees.

9. mental and emotional steadiness

   • I doubt that Thoreau would be thrown off *balance* by the fantastic sights and sounds of the 20th century.

   —E. B. White

That's a lot to digest! Better pull out some Occam's razor mojo to distill this down: we can start by removing references to equipment, finance, judgment as in free elections, and art. That helps.

What about the age-old image of the scale as in the *scales of justice?* That might make sense to some. Leaders should be 50 percent relationships and 50 percent results to keep the scale from tipping. The problem with this is that it assumes these concepts sit side by side with one another, when they don't. They actually sit one atop the other, as we'll see. This is a very important distinction. While it would be easy to visualize the Square and the Triangle next to one another, it would quickly invalidate the concept. So, take the scale concept out of your mind.

Oddly enough, definition 7 is the closest to the operational concept I'm describing—the act of physical balance. As a practitioner of martial arts, one of the concepts that was drilled into me over and over was having a solid foundation under me. Remember the cannon and the bamboo platform? To deliver a punch, I had to be on a stable, solid surface.

Try stepping away from this book for just a minute and stand on one foot. Bonus points if you can continue to read and do this. Quite impressive! Try each foot separately. At first, try standing for just a few seconds. First your right foot, then your left. Try standing for longer periods of time. Getting wiggly?

This is the best definition of balance, when thinking about the Square and the Triangle. **Each leader must be aware of his or her foundation.** When you stood on your feet, did you quickly find how one was easier than the other? How on one foot, you remained poised, with minimal rocking, while on the other foot you were reaching for something to grab to keep upright? This is the concept of *foundation,* which we'll explore in the chapter titled The Square and the Triangle.

Balance in leadership isn't about being equally good at everything. It's about foundation and adjustment.

Back to your feet once more. Try standing on both feet, separately again, and hone in on knowing which foot is truly your solid foot, the one you can stand on alone most easily.

Now, just walk around the room. You are naturally using both feet. Notice this very important point: You use both feet to move. Just because one foot, or leg more aptly, is better adapted to *balancing* your body alone, doesn't mean that you solely rely on it. Put another way, you're not going to give up walking and, instead, hop around on your good leg.

You won't lead with only the Square or the Triangle. However, in those moments when you need your good foot, your stronger foot, isn't it nice to know which one it is? The other competency *balances* on it as you lead. Generally, they will work together, even though one might pull more weight than the other.

BALANCE IN MOTION

As you stood on your feet, both together and one at a time, I hope you recognized that you can trust your body to work as a whole. Despite one foot being steadier than the other when used singly, each has an important role to play. The key is to remember that balance isn't about being equal.

Balance is about stability, not equality.

It's about adjusting your foundation to hold up the weight you put on it.

Back to your feet one more time: this time, trying each foot separately, stand and balance on your foot. First the less natural foot, then the stronger foot (let's end on a positive, eh?). Now pay close attention to what's going on with your foot, your leg, and your body. Do you see the subtle—or not so subtle—adjustments that are taking place under you? The slight hops and jumps to remain standing, the wiggle in your hips as you move your weight around to avoid falling? Notice how with your solid foot, you likely made fewer adjustments than you needed to with your less natural foot.

Those adjustments happen with the Square *or* with the Triangle as your foundation. One of these two competencies is going to prove to be your *solid foot*—the one you balance on. You'll want to get to know it well. And ideally, if you have your solid foot under you, you'll need to make fewer adjustments.

Adjustment is the key to balancing. This will be true for your leadership, just as with staying on your feet. When you watch any sport that truly requires balance, think gymnastics or figure skating for example, watch how the athlete has to occasionally fight to regain his or her balance? Those little wobbles after a jump or an ambitious maneuver come about when the athlete's base isn't truly spot-on. Even with world-class athletes, you'll see those little adjustments. If you watch me try to "stick a landing," you'll see what wobbling *really* looks like.

Watch a plate-spinning performer at a circus sometime. If you don't know what I'm talking about, it's that person (usually a clown) with the dinner plate literally spinning while suspended atop a long stick. The clown sets the plate spinning at high speed on the stick (with the narrowest of contact points), while balancing it in place. And the good performers are spinning multiple plates at one time.

Watch their foundation carefully—which is their whole body when they are balancing a plate. See the micro-adjustments that take place to keep the plate in the air? The clown has to be constantly observing and adjusting to keep the plate from falling. Those adjustments are the key to maintaining the balance. It's just as true for leadership as it is for spinning plates.

When you look at pictures of the Square and the Triangle, you're looking at fixed shapes. It can be easy to forget that these pictures really represent activity in motion. You won't build and leverage relationships in a static way—they take interaction. And results don't just happen—they take action too. As you begin to explore your own Square and Triangle, this will become more apparent. You'll begin to see how your balance gets shaky, just like when you stood on your weaker foot.

With the Square and the Triangle, those micro-adjustments will separate your good leadership moments from your weaker ones. In managing your relationships, you come to know the people around you and what makes them tick. You also come to know their moods and sensitivities. On any given day, you'll adjust to make sure you can get the most from the people around you.

Results will be no different. Things happen in the business world that can derail your outcomes. Sometimes it's people, sometimes it's circumstances. A shipment of product doesn't arrive on time. Weather forces the cancellation of a meeting. A computer breaks down. People leave—people you were counting on.

Things happen that force you to adjust so you won't be knocked off balance. In many cases, what happens to your Square will affect your Triangle and vice versa. Knowing how to adjust either is critical to keeping them in balance.

BE AWARE OF YOUR BASE

It is important to know that you will still need to practice both Square and Triangle competencies. If you want to get really good at balancing, you can't always practice with your good foot. To use another bicycle analogy, cyclists, especially those who use the clipless pedals, must learn a lot about balance. Otherwise they can get stuck in the pedal, tip over, and crash to the ground. Cyclists quickly learn which foot they like to remove from the pedals first. They put that foot down for stabilization when coming to a stop—to avoid falling over. This good foot is known in some circles as your *chocolate foot*. I have no idea where that phrase comes from, but I like it.

Cyclists get to know their chocolate foot well. They use it a lot. Inevitably though, the day comes when you need to pull out the other foot in an emergency. And cyclists who haven't practiced how to do that tend to fall. It's a painful lesson about why you can't solely rely on your good foot. *You need them both.* Falling off a bike is embarrassing, usually painful, and sometimes causes serious injury.

Falling in leadership can be equally embarrassing and painful. Understanding balance can most certainly help you when the ground is uneven beneath your feet.

In the case of leadership, instead of a right and left foot, you have relationships and results—the Square and the Triangle. You'll need to have both to be truly successful in the long term. Unlike your feet, they won't stand side by side, but they will work with each other; the one you are best at will form your base or your foundation.

TAKE-HOME MESSAGES

△ Balance keeps you and your leadership upright.

△ Balance requires you to be aware of your base.

△ Staying balanced requires adjustment.

SECTION II

The Square and
the Triangle

4

The Square and the Triangle

Pictures tell a story words cannot. By visualizing relationships (Square) and results (Triangle) and how they work together, you can learn more about how you lead and how to improve.

For the first three chapters, I described the Square and the Triangle with the one-word definitions and then discussed how they relate. In this chapter, I want to introduce you to these two foundational competencies in greater detail by focusing on their shapes. I'll describe the *construct* and the concept. While remarkably simple in design, look for the depth that exists in these minimalist pictures. They are similar to a Chinese watercolor painting. Despite sometimes sparse brush work, the emotions they convey and the pictures they represent are expansive compared to the minimalist nature of the painting itself.

This doesn't conflict with the core concept of simplicity. The pictures will come to represent all of the leadership strengths and weaknesses you'll focus on as you journey toward becoming a better leader. Let's start with the surface and dive deeper in later chapters.

THE SQUARE

The Square represents *relationships*—your connection with other people. It's how you connect with others, your sociability level, and your degree of introversion or extroversion. Do you love the presence of people and do you get energy from others? Do you favor relationships above all else? There's more to this for sure, but try to see all of those ideas wrapped up in this shape.

When you see this Square, see relationships. In all forms, good or bad. Whether you favor them or not. Just connect relationships with this shape.

THE TRIANGLE

The Triangle represents results, though there's more to it than that. Results-mindedness, or results orientation, is probably a more accurate phrase. Results-oriented people are driven, urgent, and have a love of checklists and checking things off their lists. They love the numbers and check them regularly.

They also tend to drive others. They push their teams toward the goals; they're willing to push when others won't. They'll give feedback (even if done poorly). They tend to get things done. Try to see this when you look at this figure.

When you see the Triangle, see results. In all forms, good or bad. Whether you get them or you don't. Just connect results with this figure.

Yep, it's simple. Seeing it reinforces its simplicity.

Now, I want you to move from processing words to processing what you see—what you feel.

As I've mentioned, we all have a base. When you practiced standing on one leg, it was either your left leg or your right leg. I mentioned cyclists and their chocolate foot. Your base is what you balance on. One of these shapes, these competencies, is your base—the natural behavior that your leadership balances on.

THE SQUARE FOUNDATION

If you lean toward people, if relationships are your thing, then focus on the picture below.

The Square at the bottom of this figure is your base—your foundational style of leadership. You lean toward people—probably love them and put most of your energy into protecting the relationships you have with them. You likely are more apt to celebrate birthdays in the office, and you're crushed when people leave you (they leave the organization but you see it more personally). You love harmony in the workplace and are happy to engage when that harmony is disrupted.

You must balance *results*—the Triangle—on top of your Square. Remember, to lead also is to get something done. You must accomplish the job. The Triangle rests on your Square because relationships are the area you naturally gravitate toward.

THE TRIANGLE FOUNDATION

If you are a *get-it-done* type, the Triangle is your base.

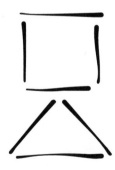

You may love counting the till at the end of the day to see how you made out. You're quick to celebrate when the job is done, done on time, and done right. You stick to deadlines (or try very hard to). The checkmark on a list might as well be a smiling emoticon. Crossing the finish line matters to you. You're also quick to push and pull the team to get there with you. When people leave your team, you might be more apt to agree that they weren't cut out for this line of work or that where they are going is a better fit—you won't take it personally. Drama is the enemy of success and you don't put up with it. Maybe you even ignore it because it takes away from focusing on outcomes.

You must balance *relationships* on top of the results you so greatly prize. Does that Square sitting up there look stable to you, or does it look like it could come crashing down? Remember, to lead is also to support and nurture people. You probably can't get all this done yourself—although you've probably tried or told yourself it would be easier and faster if you could.

Look at these two competency combinations side by side:

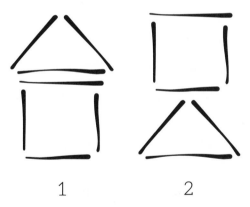

Does one seem stronger to you? More stable? I've numbered them 1 and 2, but that's not because one is preferred or more common.

It would be easy to say the first picture with relationships on the bottom is more stable. That it's *better*—just look at that second picture. That Square could fall at any time.

However, assessing these pictures in that way would be doing a real disservice to both of them. Remember the key concepts. There are only two competencies you need: *relationships* and *results*. They must be in balance with one another. One must hold the other up, and you need to be aware of your base—your natural behavior.

Let's pick on the people (nicely) who are represented by figure 1. While it might look stable, there are risk points that appear regularly for leaders in this category. One of the managers I taught this to called this figure *the house*. I liked it. Thank you.

The house seems great. It evokes warmth, comfort, family, and security. "People" people will love the imagery of great collegial relationships and the comfort in being around people you want to work with. The issue with the house analogy is that, if ignored, the Triangle has the potential to be a leaky roof. I've worked with a lot of people-oriented leaders who just loved their teams. Some were exceptional, but many fell into some common traps. Tell me if this sounds familiar:

"I like my manager but we never really get clear direction."

"She's super nice. But I can't always count on her to tell me what to do."

"I wish he'd give me feedback I can do something with—he never really seems to say what's on his mind."

"I like him but I can't say I respect him."

"Can't we just get some work done?"

The Square managers are generally great with their people but many of them fail to capitalize on how good their relationships are. They just don't seem to be able or willing to test the relationship. Remember the cannon and the bamboo platform?

What good is building a stone platform if you never put a cannon on it?

Just because you're a relationship person doesn't guarantee that you're going to be any better off than a more uptight, get-it-done type.

Okay, the Triangle people are now feeling a bit smug. Maybe it pays to get stuff accomplished after all. Well, hang on. Look at figure 2 again. It looks unstable for a reason. Results are just fine—they're more than fine. They're what somebody hired you to achieve. But you can't do it without other people. Just listen to these tidbits:

"My boss is a little short on providing praise."

"I never hear when I do well, just when I screw up."

"I don't know why celebrating a birthday has to be seen as loafing."

"My boss is a jerk."

If you focus on results at the expense of your people, I can assure you, you'll be getting short-term gains only. And eventually, no gains. You'll be plagued by turnover and find it increasingly hard to accomplish much of anything. And if you fall into the trap of blaming your staff, you'll get further and further behind. Results can't come at the cost of your people.

Is there hope for either of you, softy Square or hard-nosed Triangle?

Yes, there is. The Square and the Triangle work as a team. You need them both. The beauty in this is that either model works. It's simply a case of getting to know which one you are and making those subtle adjustments that keep them properly balanced.

TAKE-HOME MESSAGES

⬜ The Square represents relationships.

△ The Triangle represents results.

△ Pictures tell stories words cannot.

5

Strengths and Weaknesses Reimagined

In management terms, strengths and weaknesses aren't very helpful terms. What you really need to know isn't your strengths or weaknesses but what comes naturally and what doesn't. Doing what comes naturally can help you offset what feels unnatural.

The Square and the Triangle are the two building blocks you need if you're going to be a successful leader—the two competencies you need to balance, no matter which one you favor. You likely have a *natural* inclination toward one over the other. While you need them both, one (more than the other) may resonate with you or with others when they think of you.

Before you dive into the Square and the Triangle details, I want to address the concept of strength and weakness.

Leadership development these days tends to be strongly tied to the words *strength* and *weakness*. Some people prefer *opportunity* rather than weakness as a more acceptable phrase, but the resulting meaning is the same. Personally, I don't like the terms. They create a value judgment that I think most people shy away from. We certainly weren't raised to discuss how weak we are.

Feats of strength are prized while weaknesses are best kept quiet. It becomes synonymous with *good* and *bad*. This kind of judgmental language, in my experience, does more to hinder leadership development than it does to encourage it. Despite the growing tendency in leadership training to emphasize leading with your strengths, it still creates the same negative feeling that part of you isn't good enough.

Leadership development strategies that quantify one's faults have done more damage to the leaders I know by discouraging them from being introspective, which is exactly what those leadership development models were hoping to encourage. The cold hard facts about our talents don't outweigh how we *feel* about our talents. No one likes to look that deeply in the mirror. It's too defeating.

With that said, it will not be possible for me to eliminate these words. The terms strengths and weaknesses are just too commonplace—and simple—to replace them. Doing so could create needless confusion. I've been controversial enough by just introducing the Square and the Triangle with their promised simplicity. However, like the Square and the Triangle, I would like to create a different picture in your mind when you hear the words *strengths* and *weaknesses*.

STRENGTH IS NATURAL

Instead of thinking about strengths and weaknesses, I'd like you to mentally replace those words with *natural* and *unnatural*. As you make this mental replacement, do your best to take good/bad, strong/weak *judgments* out of your mind. You need to feel good about your leadership journey, encouraged as you take each step—rather than throwing your hands in the air and giving up.

Let me start by describing what a strength is. Do you know how some things just come easily for you? Think of your schooling; remember those classes you took where the material just seemed easy to learn? Maybe so much so that you didn't bother to read the book or study for the test. You just showed up, got a great grade, and went about your day. The homework was a piece of cake and you didn't have a care in the world about the subject. We're talking easy A.

I'm not saying you liked the subject, it just came easy for you. I know lots of people who are good at things but don't necessarily enjoy doing them. Strength in this context has more to do with things coming naturally versus being *good*. They're more like a *default*—it's there whether you want it or not.

WEAKNESS IS UNNATURAL

Weaknesses represent abilities that don't come naturally, as opposed to something you're just flat not good at. Back to school: there were classes you took that required every bit of effort you had, even if you got good grades. You studied more, you stressed more, and you never really felt confident. For me, math was this subject. I got great grades in math, but I worked for every decimal place (pun intended). It just never came naturally for me so it took a lot more effort. If I didn't give it that effort, my grades could have easily suffered. Let's call this the hard A.

Leadership and school are similar. They're both about choices. Even when it's hard, if you choose to do something well, chances are you can do it but at what expense? The personal energy it takes to be effective at something that isn't natural can be exhausting.

Think about the Square. I've never met a leader who couldn't relate to people. Not once. On the other hand, I've met lots of leaders who *chose* not to relate to people. Maybe they chose not to because they didn't want to or maybe they chose not to due to shyness. Or some other reason. In any case, the failure to relate to someone wasn't about their ability to do so.

For the natural "people" people, relating to others comes so easy for them, they almost can't explain why they can do it. Just like the mathematics superstars I know, not one of them could explain *why* they were so good in math. They just were. For the *unnatural* people leaders, connecting to others wasn't something they were incapable of, it was just not a natural tendency. In fact, I've watched many of them do it and do it well. However, because it didn't come naturally, it could be very draining on them.

UNNATURAL IS NOT INSURMOUNTABLE

Don't apply judgment to your notion of strengths and weaknesses. It's very disheartening to believe you are incapable of something. For those natural strength points, the goal is to find ways to benefit from them, maybe more than you already are. As for those draining, unnatural moments, the key is to find ways to be effective while not taxing yourself needlessly. Trust me, you can do this. How you get there will vary based on who you are. The key is to remove the stigma that comes with judgment. As soon as you recognize you are a capable leader and have a plan to utilize your skills, you're going to make greater leaps in your development than you might believe possible.

So, while you're going to read a lot about strengths and weaknesses going forward, please know that those words are being used simply due to the prevalence in today's leadership language. Repeat after me: *strength equals natural* and *weakness equals unnatural.* It doesn't mean capable or incapable.

UTILIZING NATURAL TALENTS

One last concept I want to cover is the "utilization" of your natural talents. Your foundation is largely determined by what will come most naturally to you. If relationships resonate with you over results, you'll more naturally focus on them and the skills surrounding them than you might with results. The same applies to results. Results-minded leaders will likely focus more on those results-related skill sets than relationships.

Utilizing your natural talents comes with its own form of balance.

75

It's possible to either underutilize or overutilize your abilities. Both can be problematic. It's important that you rely on your talents at the right times and in the right amount to be successful.

Given that natural talents come more easily, there can be a tendency to over-rely on them. If being courageous and driving your team comes naturally, you have to be cautious not to overdo it. An overused strength can cause you grief, despite how natural it might feel.

Conversely, an underutilized talent can be equally damaging. You might have a talent for networking and knowing your people, but if you hold yourself back and fail to take advantage of that ability, you might also fail to be successful. As weird as this sounds, just because you have a natural comfort with something doesn't mean you'll always use it. I've seen leaders hold themselves back from using their talents as a way to avoid overutilization, and in turn, they fail to "do that thing they do well" often enough.

Utilization can affect your weak or unnatural areas as well. Underutilizing a weak area is pretty obvious. You might shy away from doing something you're not comfortable with. However, it's possible to overutilize a weak area as well. Think in terms of overcompensating—trying too hard to do something well that doesn't come naturally. This is important to consider as you assess your developmental needs.

Keep utilization in mind as you read more about the Square and the Triangle.

TAKE-HOME MESSAGES

△ *Strength* and *weakness* create negative reinforcement.

△ *Natural* and *unnatural* are more motivating and accurate.

△ If you over- or underutilize your talents, you won't lead effectively.

6

The Square

The Square is all about relationships. It is a vital part of leadership. With it, you will develop authentic and engaging connections that will help you achieve successful outcomes.

Leadership is all about the balance struck between relationships and results. In this chapter, we'll look at the Square—the relationships. Relationships are an important component to your success as leader. As you begin to recognize the power inherent in relationships, it's important to know how to harness that strength. We'll take a deeper look at what goes into your Square foundation and then we'll look closely at the strengths that come from Square leadership and some of the pitfalls or weaknesses that can come from not having a handle on how to lead from the Square. Just because the Square is your foundation doesn't mean you can take it for granted.

While this chapter is dedicated to the Square and aimed at Square-minded leaders, Triangle-minded leaders should not skip it. The pitfalls of a weak Square can affect you. Given that it isn't your natural leaning, you need to recognize the difficulties produced by a weak Square. You'll have to balance this out with your Triangle. With better self-awareness and understanding, even those who are more rooted in the Triangle will be able to lead relationships more effectively.

WHAT'S IN A SQUARE?

Relationships Defined

The Square represents relationships. It is important to know what relationships are, how they're formed, and how to leverage them.

So, what are relationships anyway, and why are they so important in your life? Relationships are, at the most basic level, the literal connections you have with other people. Unless you work completely on your own and are your own customer, you have relationships. Here are just some of them:

- Your boss
- Your peers
- Your subordinates
- Your customers
- Your vendors or shared partners
- Your business community

Your list may be longer, but it's likely these are all people you need to be aware of and interact with to achieve results.

Every one of these relationships comes with its own set of needs. The relationship you have with your boss likely looks different than the one you have with your subordinates. You're dependent upon your boss for direction. Your employees are dependent upon *you* for direction. With that said, even though you depend on your boss for guidance, you still have a role in shaping that relationship. It's not one-way. You will need to influence your boss on deadlines, unclear expectations, targets you can't reach, etc. It isn't always comfortable to do, but it must be done.

Your subordinates depend on you in the same way. They will be looking to you for guidance. You will need to shape your relationship with them with similar thinking, albeit with role reversal.

Think about how you like to be led.

Can you, in turn, provide that to your people?

Peer relationships are equally important. Unlike the relationships with your boss or your subordinates, neither party in a peer relationship has *authority* over the other. Consequently, the way you influence one another changes. This can create an uncomfortable dynamic for some. Speaking for myself, I always found this the hardest group to provide feedback to. These people were my work *friends,* so being direct with them wasn't always as easy as it was with my direct reports.

It's a great thing to take stock of. Which relationships come easy for you? Which don't?

The list goes on and on. Do you deal with a board of directors? Do you have shareholders? What about stakeholders in your business who don't work for you, like contractors or vendors? Your customers are some of the most important stakeholders you work with. When you look at it, you are literally surrounded by people you need to interact with and influence. You have to keep your relationships fully in view if you're going to be the kind of leader that people want to follow.

Relationship Lifecycle

Relationships are more than the identifiable intersections between people. Relationships have a natural lifecycle that should be understood and managed. Relationships have a beginning— they must be formed—a middle, the *life* of the relationship, and occasionally they have ends, planned or otherwise. How you lead in these phases is important and being aware of where you are in the lifecycle will help you adjust.

Early on, relationships need to be formed. This occurs when you hire a new employee, when you yourself are hired, or when you meet a new customer. It occurs when others get hired on your team. It occurs when you get introduced to your new boss. Recognizing the formation of a relationship is important. These are important moments in which you'll need to build an effective base you can lead from later.

Once established, relationships mature and arrive at the middle of the lifecycle. You've reached a point in which real work can occur. You depend on one another and, as a leader, you should be actively influencing the people around you. In this period, you must be properly aware at all times of the health of the relationship. You will be nurturing it, checking in on it, and leveraging it. It's a critical time because it is in these moments you will achieve results while working with the other person. This is the coaching and mentoring phase. Many leaders fail to maintain a relationship they've worked hard to build. Don't be that leader. If you don't protect it, you won't be able to benefit from it.

Occasionally relationships end. It may be by choice or happenstance. This is important to recognize as well. Should you choose to end a relationship, as when you need to terminate employment, doing so with dignity is important to your leadership brand. Termination can be done sensitively and with minimal harm. When endings occur through retirements or resignations, you have a window, sometimes short, to benefit from what the person leaving can share with you. Leveraging endings can be important for helping you answer the question, where do we go from here? Done well, it doesn't have to be catastrophic when someone leaves your team.

Relationships can end because of you. One theme that is very consistent in turnover data is that a major reason, sometimes the number one reason, why people leave a job is because of their boss. Are you leading in a way that ends relationships? Are people choosing to leave because of you? If so, you need to get an immediate handle on this situation. You *need* your people. Lead so that they want to work with you rather than want to get away from you.

Be aware of the lifecycle and where you are in it. It dictates how you need to lead.

Protecting and Leveraging Relationships

Relationships must be protected and leveraged. You've made an investment with a new person. It's important to protect the return on that investment. Ensuring that the other person sees the value you place in the relationship is critical to protecting it. You must protect a relationship with integrity. It can't just be a means to an end. If people assume you don't really care about them but just about the results they can achieve, you won't be seen as protecting the relationship.

Protection comes in many forms, but it's ultimately about building trust, caring for the other person, and having their best interests at heart. If you do these things, not only will you be able to leverage the relationship, they'll respond to you when you do.

Leveraging the relationship is all about benefitting from the relationship for both parties, not taking advantage of it. It's about knowing the other person's abilities and putting them to work. It's about growing those talents so that the person becomes increasingly valuable. When you know a person's talents and readiness to grow, you'll find great ways to stretch them safely, taking them where they might be nervous to go but where the fear of falling is limited.

By protecting and leveraging relationships, you'll ensure your people will be there to reach outcomes today and tomorrow.

A STRONG SQUARE

The Square foundation is an important vehicle to ensuring your leadership success. Those leaders who know this and take advantage of it can benefit greatly. Done well, the Square-focused leader will exhibit a number of qualities, including knowing their people, being better change agents, driving improved engagement, and generating an authentic feel that people will want to follow.

Knowing Your People

I've had the good fortune of watching some leaders who really understood the need to get to know their people. Taking time to get to know someone, care for them, and look out for them is critical if you want someone to follow you.

I worked with a CEO who truly understood this. Despite his C-suite or "suit" position, the people around him, from all levels in the organization, really gravitated to this guy. He had a knack for getting to know people, I mean really *know* them, that was as good as any I've seen. He made a real effort to learn names, remember them, and to remember something about every person. I never stopped being amazed at how he could remember someone's name and their backstory months after the original introduction. The employees loved it, and they adored him. He was seen as approachable and real.

Because he was so good at this, he was able to truly leverage those around him. He had high expectations, but people would follow him. It was particularly evident at the staff level. Where employees would typically flee from a CEO, let alone want to work with upper management, this CEO's ability to connect with others was a natural draw when he needed a volunteer.

Leaders who recognize people as people, who take the time to connect on a human level and not just as an asset, can benefit from this. This is a clear advantage when leading from the Square foundation. This is a critical aspect of the Square skills that Triangle-minded leaders should work to achieve.

Change Agent

Change management is hard. Trust me. Look at the number of books on the subject as an indicator of this. Organizations these days experience an unbelievable amount of change. With the fast pace of changing consumer needs and the overwhelmingly short shelf life of technology, companies are under ever-increasing demands. We're all designed to enjoy a certain degree of comfort and stability. Upsetting the balance of things is disturbing and it can exhaust or kill a team. The Square skills are the secret weapons to counterbalancing this.

Change is hard on people. Knowing this, it's important to demonstrate empathy. It's also important to leverage the team's ideas as to how to approach change. By focusing on the relationships, a Square-minded leader can help to reduce the victimization and powerlessness that comes when changes occur. Further, it can create buy-in and support for the future direction. When people feel their issues have been surfaced and heard, it can help them move through their own feelings and find the value in what's new, not just for themselves but for the organization.

Engagement

If you want to drive employee engagement, you won't likely do it without focusing on the employees themselves. I've seen a lot of engagement strategies fail because leaders failed to look through the eyes of their employees.

I helped one manager at a company totally change her relationship with her team through a simple solution aimed at driving connection. This leader was liked by her employees generally, but their support was beginning to fade. Her staff worked in a processing lab that was around the corner from her office. In turn, her office was located near a back door that led to the administrative hall. This leader made a habit of walking from her office to the hall through this door, bypassing her work area and her people. When assessing the situation, I recommended to her that she no longer use the back door and only enter and exit through the processing lab.

The result was remarkable. And simple. She saw her people more often, engaged with them more often, and her credibility popped right back up. Taking her own convenience off the table and replacing it with visibility to her team did the trick.

Employee engagement is a hot topic in human resources and management circles. A lot has been said about how to understand it and improve on it. Square leadership done well plays an enormous role in understanding the culture of your team and leading through it. When your teams feel supported and understood, they will feel connected. With that sense of purpose, they will *want* to put their talents to work for the greater good of the organization.

Your relationship with your staff isn't solely about accomplishing the job. It's also about creating the culture in which your staff will perform.

High-performing teams come from creating relationships and cultures that foster joy in the work and the workplace.

The emotional uplift that comes from good relationships goes a long way.

Authenticity

Another strength realized from the Square skill set is authenticity. Leading strongly in this way generally produces better interpersonal connection and communication. Leading this way lets you "hook" people on a personal level that garners attention and trust.

Have you ever been to a group meeting or organization-wide event in which a senior leader tells you how much he or she appreciates all you do? Think about the ones who poured on the syrup (or didn't) and you just felt inclined to tune him or her out. The person didn't seem genuine, didn't *mean* what he or she was saying. We've all watched a senior leader who lacked this Square tendency try to praise a group and actually turn the audience off! Praise that feels contrived won't resonate with your audience.

Alternatively, think about a leader who said something similar that resonated with you. In many cases the words were the same but there was that *something* that was different. Close your eyes—you can see and hear it now. When that person thanked the organization, you believed it! For the best leaders, it's not about the words or the delivery. It's about the authenticity. When people really love people, you can just feel it. It shows.

A WEAK SQUARE

There are obvious benefits to honing the Square foundation and leading from it. Equally, though, there are some pitfalls to either not using the Square skills enough or failing to develop them. These pitfalls can commonly plague leaders who identify with the Triangle foundation. Given that the Square isn't natural for them, it's not unusual for these issues to appear.

However, it can occasionally affect Square leaders too. This may come as a surprise. It comes back to utilization—if you're not relying on your skill set often enough, you may not benefit from your Square foundation the way you should be able to.

When the Square foundation isn't leveraged or well understood, it can create a number of problems, including an inability to connect with others, failure to properly include others, and a general failure to leverage relationships due to fear.

Inability to Connect

When a leader doesn't have natural skill in the Square or isn't aware of its importance, it can have an effect on the relationships around him or her. It probably sounds obvious that a person who doesn't lead through relationships isn't going to benefit from them. I believe there is more to it than that, though.

If you don't take time to connect with others, you won't be able to leverage what they can do for you. It's possible for this to happen to people who are relationship-oriented. Embarrassment and self-esteem issues can play a role. I know a number of leaders who are too embarrassed to learn from and leverage the people around them, despite being more Square-minded. Their own personal anxieties prevent them from being vulnerable with others. Consequently, they don't connect on a deeper level with their teams and don't gain the advantages these people bring—advantages that might offset their personal fears. As a result, they fail to lean into their relationships as a safety net and place of personal growth.

If you've taken time to build trust in a relationship, it's important to demonstrate vulnerability with those you've connected with. It goes a long way to establishing trust.

Failure to Include Others

While leaders with strong Squares really know and leverage their teams, a weak Square can result in the opposite experience—a failure to include others.

This can occur when a leader hasn't taken the time to know the team's abilities. That place of ignorance can cause a leader to do the work herself because she doesn't know what people are capable of. Embarrassment can get in the way, too. Just as it affects making the connection in the first place, it can prevent inclusion when self-esteem gets in the way. I worked with a leader who was embarrassed to add people to her teams because she felt she'd look inferior. Despite knowing the value of others, embarrassment prevented her from surrounding herself with talent.

When you yield to embarrassment, you literally fail to take advantage of the relationships you have.

Fear of Ruining a Relationship

By far, one of the biggest weaknesses I've seen develop in the Square leader is fear of damaging a relationship and losing it. When people build relationships and fail to use them out of fear of loss, it's tragic. This goes beyond personal embarrassment. It is the fear of *losing* the relationship as opposed to looking weak or ineffective.

By way of example, let me share an analogy through children. If you're a parent, this might sound familiar. You have a child who is extremely social. He loves having friends and knows all the kids on the block. One of his friends is a little mischievous. He'll play with things he's been told are off-limits (like your computer), knows where the cookie jar is and raids it willingly, and has a tendency to get in trouble. Your son goes along with him and takes the cookies and plays with the computer because his friend encourages it. You find out (you always find out) and you ask your son why he broke the rules? Your son says, "He is my friend—I don't want him not to like me!" Aargh!

Your son had difficulty saying, "No—we can't do this," for fear of losing his friend. Fear of losing the relationship outweighed doing and saying what he knew was right.

Leaders make this same mistake. They fail to coach and mentor because they are afraid of damaging the relationship. "If I push my team too hard, they won't follow me." Meaning, they won't like me.

I worked with a leader who was solidly rooted in the Square. He suffered from this very problem. He was so protective of his relationships, he was afraid to tax them. Remember, the goal of the Square is to build relationships that tolerate the weight we put on them. He and I spoke about his inability to give feedback to his team and I told him that his failure to talk to his people bordered on selfishness. He was hurt by the remark (I felt bad about it afterwards) and confused. I softened the blow by telling him that because he was so worried about losing his relationships, he was robbing his staff of his guidance. I told him that he appeared more protective of his reputation than the relationship.

Fortunately, he looked within himself and asked his staff about my remarks. While they said it better and kinder than I had, he heard the same thing. They *wanted* him to coach them. They *wanted* to please him. When he started doing so, his relationships got stronger. He thanked me for it later, and I apologized for being too blunt.

UTILIZATION ISSUES

Difficulty within the Square often comes from utilization issues—failing to consider the Square enough or leading with too heavy an emphasis on it. When you either underuse or overuse the Square, problems can develop. Underuse is generally more common for Triangle-minded leaders but I've seen it with Square-minded ones occasionally. Examples of utilization issues include:

- **Too much emphasis on relationship-building:** Square leaders are relationship-centric. However, when you spend more time on building relationships and not enough on leveraging them, you'll fail to benefit from them. Ask yourself, what are you gaining from the relationships you've built? Can you tie results to them? If not, you might be overly focused on building. *Overused Square*

- **Too much focus on "team":** If you spend too much time praising the team and not enough time praising individuals, you could find your staff not feeling recognized despite your efforts. Teamwork is important, but individuals want to know their contribution mattered. Don't overlook your superstars while trying to preserve teamwork. Praise has to be precise, not just high volume. *Overused Square*

- **Failure to recognize and praise:** "Do we do anything right?" Misapplied praise can hurt you as a leader. So can failing to recognize the people on your team and the quality of their work altogether. Even if things are getting done to your satisfaction, your people need to know it. If your team doesn't believe you recognize them, you won't likely keep your team. *Underused Square*

- **Failure to grow your team:** If you find that you only give work to certain members of your team (they are the only ones you "trust") or your whole team isn't as capable as you need them to be, the problem might be you. When you fail to delegate, to teach, and to provide opportunity, you're ultimately failing to recognize that you need *all* of your people in order to succeed. Without them, you won't get results. ***Underused Square***

What Does This Look Like?

As noted, weakness in the Square generally comes from not being aware of or sensitive enough to relationships. Without them, you won't produce results. This is true regardless of your foundation, whether it's Square or Triangle.

This can be easily seen through pictures:

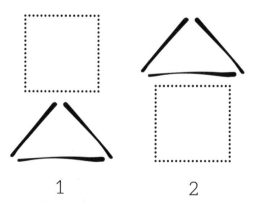

Figure 1 shows a leader with a Triangle foundation who struggles with the unnatural tendencies he or she faces with relationships. Figure 2 shows a Square-rooted leader who might not be fully utilizing the relationships he or she has. The natural tendency is to lean toward people, but the willingness to leverage them isn't quite developed.

For leaders finding themselves resonating with figure 1, take stock of what you do well in getting results that can tie to people. As an example, are you a planner? Plan with *people* in mind, not just results. Look to chapter 8, specifically the section called Integrating Your Triangle into the Square, for more details on putting your foundation to work for you.

For leaders who are nodding their head at figure 2, how can you truly take advantage of what you do well with people? For starters, "go with it"—that Square is your foundation for a reason. Don't be afraid to use it. Also, look within and ask yourself why are you holding back? Getting feedback from your team can help motivate you. Chances are they want to follow you. This chapter should help to provide you with insights as to how to leverage your Square. Reread both A Strong Square and A Weak Square sections to get a good picture of what success looks like. Then review the Utilization Issues section to be sure you're maximizing your abilities rather than failing to use them.

Being aware of where you are in this Square continuum is important for devising strategies to help you develop further.

TAKE -HOME MESSAGES

- ☐ Square leadership lets you build, protect, and leverage people.
- ☐ A strong Square foundation allows you to manage change and engage others.
- ☐ A weak Square foundation results in limited connections and leverage.

7

The Triangle

The Triangle is about results. It is a vital part of leadership. With it, you'll develop high-quality, mission-oriented teams who know how to get things done.

Relationships are balanced by results. Leadership is as much about outcomes as it is about people. The power found in the Triangle is about leading to outcomes. Keeping your teams on track and on schedule is where the Triangle shines. As with the Square, we'll look at the strength found in the Triangle foundation. We'll also see the weaknesses that can develop. Just because the Triangle is your foundation doesn't mean you can take it for granted.

While this chapter is aimed at Triangle-rooted leaders, Square-minded leaders need to pay attention to this chapter too—in particular, the weaknesses that can develop. Given that this may not feel natural to you, you could be more susceptible to the weak areas. Being more self-aware of this will help you find ways to lead with greater results. Again, it's about balance.

WHAT'S IN A TRIANGLE?

The Triangle is a powerful part of leadership and the counterpart to your Square. It's about results and what it takes to get results.

Let's begin by looking at what I mean by results.

What Is a Result?

Results are the product of effort. You take action and something *results*. Ideally, it's an outcome you expected, but results can be unexpected as well. This is true in work and in daily life. Exercise is a good example. Lifting weights in the gym *results* in stronger muscles.

Another way to put this is *cause and effect*. When you act, something occurs. There is an effect that occurs related to the cause that induced it. This is important in leadership because we want our *causes* to be purposeful and tied to a predictable *effect*.

Results are measurable. Deadlines, goals, quotas, profit. You name it. Results shouldn't be random. You should know what you're trying to accomplish. It's important to be able to measure a result so that you can ensure it's the right result.

Measurement includes a number of factors. The classic approach is the SMART approach: Specific, Measurable, Achievable, Relevant, Timely. In essence, measurements are built around the realistic nature of the project and the project's relevance to your work (why work on something with no meaning to you?). The measurement should include a data set that helps you know what you're achieving, both along the way and in the end. If you don't approach goals in this or a similar fashion, you're likely to end up with outcomes you didn't plan for.

Results Are Behavioral

Results as seen through the Triangle viewpoint aren't just a set of data. The Triangle is ultimately about the leadership behavior you need to demonstrate to ensure results are reached.

Remember, you're leading others and leading *through* others toward the goal, not just yourself.

Triangle leadership embodies a number of concepts, including planning, urgency, critical thinking, and courage. Think of these as elements within the Triangle rather than separately. When you look at and think about the Triangle leadership approach, see how these concepts interact.

Planning is the act of looking over the work and ensuring you know in advance what is going to happen and who is going to do it. It also includes understanding the timing of activity.

Urgency is the will to get the work done. A great plan is like a road map. The map won't take you anywhere. It just tells you where to go. Urgency is the act of getting in the car, turning it on, and pressing the gas. You need to have the willpower to see work through to completion.

Critical thinking is that ability to see the work from all angles and also see how to adapt. Do you know the effect of your work, who will it impact, and who needs to be included or updated? You can't just blindly go about work. The road map might have been well designed, but what happens when you find out the road ahead is closed? Critical thinking helps with planning, but it's equally important when the plan doesn't hold up.

Courage is your willingness to manage through your people. Giving feedback is a common example. Telling people when things aren't going according to plan or when an individual isn't performing up to par takes courage. It's not easy for most people, but to lead effectively through the Triangle, it's absolutely necessary.

A STRONG TRIANGLE

When used well, the Triangle is your source of strength in leading to an outcome.

Getting results is mostly about leading others through to the end.

Outside of your own personal need to succeed, the Triangle-minded person leads others to execute the plan. Those who have a solid understanding and grasp of the Triangle demonstrate this strength in a number of ways, including mission orientation, drive, talent management, and thinking on the spot.

Mission Orientation

It's extremely hard to succeed if you don't know where you're going. What the best Triangle leaders do well is establish the mission and keep everyone clear on it. These leaders know how high to jump and when to do it. They go to great lengths to ensure there is no ambiguity in the goal or in the plan to get there. When teams don't know where they're going, results suffer. Triangle leadership works to avoid any confusion about the goal.

Planning is a part of mission orientation. When you know where you're headed, you'll be inspired to plan the route. Great Triangle leaders get this. One method I saw used at one of my jobs was "backwards planning." It's a great technique. In essence, you start with the intended result and work backwards to determine the steps to get there. It's rather like planning your route to the restaurant by running the map backwards from there to your house.

We used it for recruiting employees. Rather than just posting want ads, we looked at the end result first. How many people did we need by when? With that goal set, we could work backwards in time to determine how many offers we needed to make (based on how many would be lost through background checks, etc.), how many interviews were required to meet the offer goal, and how many applications we'd need to fill the interview slots. It was very mathematical. The method was brilliant and one I'd never seen before. It helped us plan the workload and timing better than ever.

My wife is a senior nursing director at a medium-sized health system. She uses a phrase I like with her people: "What do you stand for?" she asks her managers. She knows that when her people have purpose and mission, their staff will know where to go. Without it, they'll perform aimlessly with no idea where they should spend their efforts or direct their thinking. Mission orientation is about momentum. Without it, you'll be stuck in place.

Drive

It's one thing to plan. It's another to execute. The best leaders know how to instill the impetus in others to get work done. There are ways to do this well and ways to do it poorly. Barking orders and pushing people is certainly a way to accomplish a task but it won't likely work for you in the long run.

Drive isn't about just telling others what to do. It's inspiring others to want to advance themselves. Leading through the Triangle is best exemplified when you help create the motivation in others who see the project or work through to the outcome.

My wife describes this routinely in her work in nursing. When nurses are at their best, they are predicting the needs of the patient by being there before the call light goes on. They make rounds on the patients and family and predict the work that's required. It's great for the patient and great for the nurse, as it allows them to control their pace. It's the job of the nursing leadership to inspire this drive or motivation.

When it doesn't work, nurses may fail to stay ahead of their work. It's a downward spiral from there. They can't stay ahead of demand, the work piles up, and the patients stop getting the best experience.

I worked with some great operational managers in the distribution world who had a great knack for keeping the work moving forward. They knew the importance of communicating the plan and helping the staff believe in it. The inspiration came through a balance of helping the employees know why the work was good for them, a friendly sense of competition, and the value of a job well done. Pride is a great motivator. Consequently, their employees got freight moved on time or early, shipped with little to no damage, and the confidence that bonus checks would reflect their effort.

Talent Management

While the Square will help you get to know your teams, the Triangle will help you with talent management. Knowing your people comes from the relationships you form—the Square. Doing something with that knowledge comes from the Triangle.

Coaching and motivating your staff is a product of courage and thoughtfulness. When you take the time to know the work you're about to engage in and what talent will be required to perform that work, you'll be better prepared to succeed. This means knowing the talent on your team and how to apply it.

Sports are filled with examples. Who is best on your team for a given situation? Coaches make replacements all the time to ensure the right player is on the field for a given situation. This is particularly true in team sports like hockey or basketball, when changes and substitutions are required based on the situation.

Driving those players to improve through the act of coaching is equally important. Just as planning and urgency go together, assessing talent and coaching talent go together. Coaching requires courage. It's easy to say, "Good game." It's harder to say, "Let me tell you how you could improve."

It's not easy for many leaders to give good, useful, action-able feedback. Your Triangle is there to help you do that. It's easier for leaders who are more naturally oriented toward their Triangle. It comes down to knowing that feedback needn't be painful and can be a source of encouragement and learning.

Focus on the growth opportunity honest feedback provides, rather than the pain it may cause.

Leaders often fail at giving feedback if they worry about hurting the other person's feelings. If you focus too much on the pain that feedback can cause, you'll rob the other person of growth. The Triangle is the source of doing it well. Talent management is about managing your people. When you actively engage in it, it will help you and your team improve, achieve outcomes, and actually protect the relationship in the future.

Thinking on the Spot

The work and the results don't always go as planned. Despite your hard work, sometimes you miss something. Sometimes things just come up. It's important to think through your plans as thoroughly as possible but not at the expense of failing to take action. There is a definite line between planning and urgency.

Now that you're moving, you need to be prepared for what can happen. Another word for this is *adaptability*.

Triangle leadership is at its best when you can stay nimble enough to react to the unforeseen. I worked with a facility manager who was skilled at this. His ability to think and act was awesome. It came from his calm demeanor—the guy just didn't get rattled. He took that calm approach to think through the issues and then devise strategies to get around the problem.

Staying cool under pressure and giving yourself the freedom to think is important when life throws you a curve ball. Leaders who can maintain their ability to think critically under pressure are the most likely to succeed when a deviation is required.

A WEAK TRIANGLE

Leading from a weak Triangle or a poorly applied Triangle can cause you quite a bit of grief. Many times, poor leadership can come from an overreliance on what one does well. This can happen easily with the Triangle. Overemphasis on the work to be done and underemphasis on managing the team can cause a lot of discord. A weak Triangle is common among Square-minded leaders, given that this isn't their more natural skill set.

Weakness in the Triangle can reveal itself in a number of ways, including disorganization, overthinking, being reactionary, or problems with managing talent and coaching appropriately.

Disorganization

Not everyone is a list writer. I know lots of leaders who have tried numerous ways to improve their personal organization and personal planning, only to end up exhausted from looking at a myriad of books, calendars, and technological promises that were supposed to keep them on track.

If you struggle with keeping on track and organizing your work, I empathize with you. It was certainly something I needed to work on too. I have generally overrelied on my ability to remember what I'm doing and where I'm going. My mental checklist was pretty good, until one day the work got more complex, my jobs got bigger, and maybe age was taking its toll. My capacity to remember it all was nearing its ceiling—and the ceiling felt like it was getting lower.

Ultimately, I overcame this by finding simple solutions to time and priority management that I stuck with. Let me emphasize *simple*. It works for Square and Triangle leadership and it works for correcting disorganization too. Don't pick a complex solution. Choose carefully and then stick with it. Changing habits is hard but it's possible.

The bad news is that if you don't get some kind of a handle on disorganization, your employees will feel it and likely suffer from your affliction. It's important that you address this if it's truly getting in the way. The good news is that this is a correctable problem. Be self-reflective and honest with yourself. Forgive yourself, and then take action.

Analysis Paralysis

One area where leaders can lose sight of their Triangle is in planning, or more aptly overplanning. For leaders who are afraid to proceed unless the plan is perfect, there is a greater chance the plan will not get off the ground. There is a time and a place for thinking through contingencies but at some point, you have to move forward.

Analysis paralysis strikes those who are afraid to fail. There's a place for nervousness. Being a little worried can keep you grounded, so you don't jump too early. However, trying to find every bump in the road will keep you from driving at all.

One of the organizations I supported suffered from this at near-epidemic levels. Planning took months when days would do, or years when months would have sufficed. The plans that were created were robust and complex and almost never started on time. It was painful to those of us who just wanted to go do something.

It had the added disadvantages of hurting morale and driving up cost. It's important to plan —the Triangle in all of us tells us so, but it has to be coupled with action or it can result in a lot of wasted time.

Jumping the Gun

Have you ever watched a running race when someone came out of the blocks before the starting gun? Being overeager to start is the natural counterpart to analysis paralysis. For the most hyper of leaders, planning is a waste of time; let's just start and we'll figure it out as we go.

Jumping the gun or being overly reactionary is just as big a problem as taking too long to plan and yet it creates the same outcomes. You go too fast, have no sense of direction, make mistakes, and then ultimately have to stop and waste time trying to figure out what you were hoping to do in the first place. The result of going too fast is, ironically, delays, dysfunction, and demoralization for the team.

The phrase "go slow to go fast" is a great countermeasure. I learned from a police-officer-turned-registered-nurse who, in his law enforcement defensive driving school, was taught this concept. In short, driving the course at break-neck speed without a seat belt was actually *slower* than driving the course at a safe speed with a seat belt. Why? The mistakes and over corrections on the course took more time than not making any at all. Also, (remember to tell your high school kids this) the seat belt helps you *drive* the car. Because you're not rocking and rolling around, you can actually put more energy into driving the vehicle and not trying to maintain your balance in the car.

Being too quick to act is an easy mistake to make. However, it's almost always going to create more work and more time in the future. Overplanning can lead to little being accomplished. So too, though, can failing to plan at all. Again, what you need is *balance*.

Feedback Struggles

As seen with the strong Triangle, giving feedback is a quality that can result in greater outcomes and opportunity for your employees. However, weak Triangles can be plagued with doing this poorly.

First off is the failure to coach due to trust issues. Some leaders hold back on giving feedback when work isn't being performed the way they'd like and just assume control of the work.

This leader doesn't trust the employee and does the work himself or gives it to someone else rather than teach.

When you believe you're better off just doing it yourself, you're on a path to working by yourself. Coaching is critical, and when you don't believe enough in others to do it, you'll hurt your results and your people.

Being afraid to deliver coaching is another problem. It's not fear of hurting others, though. This fear is more personal. I worked with a leader who didn't like to help people grow because he was afraid if his team improved, he'd be putting his job at risk. He literally held back improving people as a solution to protecting himself. What a mistake!

Fear of coaching and, consequently, failure to coach is a career killer in many organizations. It's critical that you teach and guide your team if you want results and if you want to be seen as a leader. If you don't and are still lucky enough to keep your job, you won't likely have access to any other jobs because you'll pigeonhole yourself as irreplaceable in your current job. However, I wouldn't count on that strategy for job security. Growing your people will help you achieve the outcomes you want now and in the future.

Lastly is the tendency to be too harsh with criticism. Not giving feedback is problematic. Being insulting and hurtful in your delivery is every bit as problematic. If you're a Triangle-minded leader who is so focused on outcomes that decency gets dropped or forgotten in the delivery of coaching, you're in for trouble. At a minimum, you'll likely face turnover on your team. No one wants to work for a bully. You could also face complaints and have to answer for yourself. Coaching must come with civility. Period.

UTILIZATION ISSUES

If you struggle with results, look to utilization for clues. Are you failing to lead enough through the Triangle (common for Square-minded leaders) or too much? Not all jobs require a hammer. If you use a hammer for everything, you'll likely break something. Look for clues that you're either underusing or over-using your skill set. Examples of this include these situations:

- **Difficulty coaching:** Are you afraid to give advice or coach your staff? Do you shy away from complex or difficult conversations? Being afraid to push your staff or direct traffic tends to be tied to fear of hurting the relationship. It's a common problem but a potentially debilitating one. Beyond failing to achieve results, it can create engagement problems (your good performers want the advice and are expecting you to manage the trouble spots), and legal problems (failing to manage performance can be costly if you don't do it correctly, let alone at all). *Underused Triangle*

- **Unclear expectations:** If you don't create clear plans for your team, they won't know where to go. If you suffer from disorganization or have trouble planning and communicating what to do, you're not going to get things accomplished. *Underused Triangle*

- **Overcoaching:** Some leaders find it all too easy to coach or correct. By coaching every failure, failing to demonstrate empathy for a struggling performer, or by being too dictatorial, you will quickly burn out your team and create resentment. The engagement costs of being too hard on your people can be just as debilitating as not working with them at all. ***Overused Triangle***

- **Taking over:** Some leaders can be so precise in their expectations that they don't believe others can do the work. They fail to delegate or when they do, they take the work back. Taking over will result in less work being done in the long run as you run out of personal capacity to do it. It also demonstrates to your teams that you don't trust them. ***Overused Triangle***

What Does This Look Like?

Weakness in the Triangle is tied to a failure to understand results, how to produce them, and how to ensure those around you know how to produce them. When you don't properly balance outcomes with relationships, you'll end up not having either of them. Regardless of your natural style, be aware of what can weaken the Triangle.

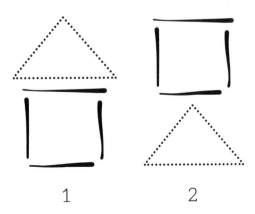

1   2

Figure 1 shows a tendency to not fully realize the potential to achieve outcomes. This can be from one's own unnatural feelings around planning and execution or a lack of driving it in others. Note that this person likely has the buy-in he or she needs; they just need to act on it. Figure 2 shows the weakness in a results-oriented person who still can't deliver. It could be from a failure to recognize the value of the team, a failure to communicate, or trying to do it all yourself.

Leaders who identify with figure 1 need to understand how their people skills can be used to get results. As an example, you know your people. How can you leverage that knowledge? Look closely at chapter 8, specifically Integrating Your Square Into the Triangle. You'll find ideas there that will help you take advantage of the connection with your people and turn them into results.

For leaders who connect with figure 2, ask yourself how you could better take advantage of your talent. Are you overdoing it and being too hard on others? Or are you failing to take advantage of your natural abilities? Reread this chapter, in particular, the sections called A Strong Triangle and A Weak Triangle, to have a clear picture on what success looks like. Then, reread the Utilization Issues section in this chapter to be sure you're taking full advantage of your abilities without overdoing it or not doing it enough.

Being very self-aware of all of this can help you develop a plan for your own growth and improvement.

TAKE-HOME MESSAGES

△ Results are measurable *and* behavioral.

△ Strong Triangle skills help you coach when needed.

△ Weak Triangle leaders may be disorganized, fail to plan, or move too fast.

SECTION III

Putting It
All Together

8

Integrating the Square
and the Triangle

*Your leadership success is rooted in how you manage
the Square and the Triangle. By leading through your
natural abilities, you can improve both how you
build relationships and achieve results.*

Leadership success is realized through both the Square and
the Triangle.

You must lead through people
to achieve results.

Generally speaking, you'll likely lean toward one or the other—people or results. Don't worry too much about to what degree this is true. Some leaders may be more naturally equal—or balanced—than others. Also, as you evolve over time, you may find a more balanced comfort level between the two. The more self-aware you become, the better the chance this will be true for you. Even if that happens, one will usually be more dominant. While I've seen leaders move between them (which they should), I've still seen enough behavioral evidence to show that one will be the more natural of the two.

If you think you're pretty *equal* in your Square and Triangle, let me share a bit of an analogy. In my own academic history, I got the same score on both my math and language sections of my SAT tests. Exactly. Despite appearing *equal*, I can assure you math was the harder section for me.

I tell you this because I think trying to determine the level of strength in one or the other is less useful than learning how to use the two together. After all, you still need both to lead.

Leaning toward one or the other can change circumstantially, however. As an example, leaders who lean more toward the Square may, under pressure, become more dominant in their Triangle. When the heat is on, we all have a tendency to drive to outcomes. Just think about a time when you were late on a deadline or had one shortened. It's easy to get results focused in those moments.

On the flip side, I've watched results-minded leaders be surprisingly people-oriented in the right situations. This was especially true in healthcare. During a number of crises I can remember, I watched some Triangle-minded leaders show surprising empathy for their people. Healthcare workers can suffer from some real compassion fatigue or grief when a bad outcome occurs. It's very difficult to watch. In those moments, these leaders just seemed to know that holding their team together was superior to asking their grieving employees a million questions about the event. That part came later.

In this chapter, I want to provide you some tips on how to use your Square or Triangle foundation to affect the other, and consequently, help you lead more effectively. As a general rule, you'll likely leverage your more natural talents over your less natural talents, but knowing how to integrate the Square and the Triangle will help you find benefit from both.

One last point of caution: the advice I'll provide below is less about leading with your *strengths* and more about balancing your leadership. I believe there is a tendency to assume that if you're leading with your strengths, you can forget about your weak areas. In my opinion, this results in lopsided leadership and frustration. You need to remain aware of your natural and unnatural areas. It's just a case of using them in concert in a way that yields success with less energy spent. It's not about ignoring the hard stuff.

INTEGRATING YOUR SQUARE INTO THE TRIANGLE

If you're a Square-rooted leader, your connection with people is likely more natural for you than the driving forces needed to achieve results. However, leading requires getting those results. By utilizing your natural "people" abilities with more purpose, you can improve the outcomes you and your team achieve. The goal is to integrate your Square (your natural comfort zone) into the Triangle (your unnatural zone).

There are a number of ways to integrate your Square into the Triangle. These include recognizing talent, building morale, and seeking feedback.

Recognizing Talent

As a strong Square leader, you likely have deep, trusting relationships with your team members. What comes with this is also a deep understanding of your team; what they like to do, what they're good at, etc. You can apply this knowledge to support achieving outcomes.

1. **Matching talent to the work:** As you learn about your team, make a list of the skills your people have and don't have. Keep them easily available. When you look at the work in front of you, take the time to assess what needs to be done and who might be best to do it. Take advantage of the relationships you've formed by benefitting from what you know about your people.

2. **Matching talent to your weak areas:** Don't be afraid to be humble. When faced with work that is challenging for you, take the time to recognize who on your team is good at something you struggle with. Make a list of your own strengths and weaknesses. Match that list to the one you created for your team. How can you benefit from the talent around you?

Building Morale

Use your ability in relationship building to help lead teams through adversity. Results don't always come easily. In periods of frustration, it's easy to get depressed and lose steam. When this happens to teams, results can suffer. When the going gets tough, the Square gets going.

1. **Matching people to the work:** Unless a project lacks nuance or layers, try to assign your team in ways that match up to their personalities and work desires. Challenging projects don't have to seem so challenging when you assign people to cohesive teams and to work they enjoy doing. Make a list of your team's professional likes and dislikes. Find ways to subdivide the work in ways that are more naturally fulfilling.

2. **Helping your team through adversity:** When difficulty strikes, lean into your Square-mindedness to help nurture your team. With your deep connection to your people, you're up to the challenge of helping the team cope when things don't go well. Take time to check up on your people. It might be as a group or one on one. Do what you do well; connect with them, listen to them, and help them realize that success is just the other side of the current bump in the road.

3. **Being generous with praise:** When things are going well, tie the current project successes and the results back to your people. Connecting them with the wins you're achieving keeps them motivated to tackle the next big project. Use "perks" or "rewards" carefully. You're not buying their allegiance, you're relating to them. Proper praise and support can be far more important than empty rewards that don't help you build relationships.

Seeking Feedback

While similar to assigning talent to support your weak spots, one of the best things you can do to support getting results is *seek* the feedback of your team. Your relationships aren't one-way. Going to your team for their ideas and suggestions builds up the relationships and yields you great information for achieving results. This is what leveraging your relationships is all about.

INTEGRATING YOUR TRIANGLE INTO THE SQUARE

Just because your root is the Triangle doesn't mean you can't have a positive impact upon relationships. You're not the only one who wants results. Your people do too. This is a common point of interest that can benefit you both. Your Triangle tendencies can actually help you enhance the relationships you need to get things done. The goal is to integrate your Triangle (your natural comfort zone) into the Square (your unnatural zone).

You can do this several ways. Use your Triangle-mindedness to help you delegate to grow, engage your teams, and enjoy victory together.

Delegate to Grow

As a planner, you need to look at work in many ways. What needs to be done? When does it need to be done? And who should do it?

Delegation is a great tool for ensuring outcomes are met. However, if you take it one step further, it can be a great developmental tool. Similar to the Square leadership style, make a list of the work that needs to be done and a list of your team's talents. Now, compare the work list to the list of your team's talents.

Look for areas in which you want to grow your team.

Assign the work with the purpose of stretching your employees, not just to get it done.

Take some risks and allow your employees to take some risks. Your job will be to observe from the background (you're a results leader, after all), but let them try their hand at something new.

You can assign the work in teams if it's too complex, but focus on growing the talent of your team.

The end result will be that the project still gets done, your team's abilities become more robust for the future, and your employees will be thankful that you took the time to invest in them.

Another cool tip I learned is to add "development" to the list of outcomes on a project. At one company I worked for, we were expected to tell the executive team tied to the project something we'd learned about our leadership during the project.

If we didn't grow while we worked, it was seen as a failure. Talk about delegating to grow. Put that on your checklist.

Plan to Engage

Speaking of checklists, I once worked with a CEO who scheduled time to write "thank-you" letters. He did so to ensure that it got done. With that in mind, how can you better engage and connect with your team if you lean toward the Triangle? You plan for it.

You're likely good at creating checklists and work schedules. With that kind of organizational talent at your fingers, try using it for "people" activities and not just tasks. Try the following:

1. Schedule one-on-one time with your staff as appropriate. Don't just assume you'll talk to them.

2. Build meeting agendas which prompt you to praise your employees and seek feedback from them.

3. Build "rounding" time on your calendar. This is literally time you carve out just to go visit your staff and see how things are going and how they are doing.

Be careful not to come across "canned" in your actions. You need to be sincere. These tips should help you when you're not naturally inclined to do these things.

Share Victory

When you reach the finish line, it's important to take time to congratulate yourself and the team. Some leaders just blindly go to the next task. Take the time—build in the time—to celebrate.

Your team wants to win too. When you build in the time to thank your team and celebrate their success, you motivate them for the next challenge ahead. Celebrating victory will further connect you with your people. Use accomplishment as a catalyst for driving relationships and further success.

When you learn to lead from your foundation (be it Square or Triangle) and integrate them, you'll be a more successful and satisfied leader.

TAKE-HOME MESSAGES

△ When you integrate the Square and Triangle leadership patterns, both improve.

▢ Use the power of your relationships to influence results.

△ Use your ability to plan and assess to support your people.

9

Strengthen Your
Square or Triangle

*Leadership is rewarding. Getting better at leadership
doesn't necessarily have to be difficult or painful.
Personal accountability will come most naturally
when you take the time to understand others,
take the time to understand yourself, and
find fun ways to approach growth.*

In the last chapter, I provided you with some ways to integrate your Square and Triangle. There are many more. When I teach the Square and the Triangle to leaders, I first work to understand their base, be it Square or Triangle, and then determine their natural/unnatural skill sets. With this understood, I can help the leader take advantage of what comes easier for him or her so they can use it to offset areas of difficulty.

Truly, no two leaders are alike. While two leaders might both be rooted in the Triangle, the individual strengths and weaknesses they have can vary. The advantage of knowing who may be Triangle-strong or Square-strong, however, makes quick work of finding mentors who can help assist you with your own growth.

Given that you're reading this book, I'll assume that you'll be undertaking part of this developmental journey on your own. There's nothing wrong with that and, frankly, it can be revealing and deeply satisfying. However, growing yourself requires some discipline. If you can, I recommend finding a mentor who can help you. I've benefitted from mentors routinely in my career, and beyond the accountability it creates, it has the added advantage of helping you see things you might miss or don't want to see.

If your mentor doesn't know about the Square and the Triangle, you can still benefit from that person. Just translate the advice by asking yourself if it pertains to relationships or results. You can use the book to further flesh out how the advice you get fits into your leadership profile.

In this chapter, I want to describe some concepts—some attitudes or perspectives—that can make this self-discovery more successful for you. Growing yourself requires being accountable to yourself. It also requires being vulnerable and recognizing the importance of perception—yours and others'. Lastly, I believe it requires a sense of joy. Learning shouldn't have to be painful. In fact, when learning is fun, you're more likely to engage in it.

ACCOUNTABILITY

If you're going to grow, being disciplined enough to do so is critical. It's no different than being in school. You have to read the book, do the homework, and study, if you're going to pass the test. Being accountable is as simple as committing to your own development and performance and following through. It also requires that you be open-minded to what you hear or learn about yourself.

There are no real secrets to this. You'll need to find a personal way that helps encourage you to stick with it. If you're working with a mentor or partner, that really helps. If you're going solo, here are some ideas to help you hold yourself accountable. You can use some or all of them:

- **Schedule time for development:** Literally put it on your calendar. Don't assume you'll have time to develop. Make the time. A planned 30 minutes once a week to reflect and plan is better than assuming you'll get to it. In my experience, you won't get to it.

- **Journal:** One of my prior coaches is rolling her eyes right now. I had a really hard time doing this. Here's the deal, though—it works. Whether you just make a few notes or literally write out a narrative, putting experiences down on paper gives you something to go back to and helps you continue to look forward.

- **Make growth visible:** I had a white board in my office. I put my developmental activities and goals on it, for everyone to see. Having it in plain view made it hard to miss and let the people around me know what I was up to. It works.

- **Build it into your work:** Don't create extra work for yourself. Find ways to develop within the work you're already doing. Avoid special projects just for development's sake. Use your current meetings, assignments, and general work as your laboratory. Anything extra will get dropped first under pressure. If it's "built in," you'll stick with it.

- **Make it simple:** If you haven't figured me out by now, let me assure you, I like simple solutions. Anything too complicated is hard to stick with. Whatever your methods, they should be fast, easy, and effective. If they're not, don't keep "recommitting" to them. Retool them until they're easy.

- **Forgive yourself:** Growth can be difficult and time consuming. Don't beat yourself up if you fall off the wagon from time to time. Forgive yourself, then take stock of the situation and recommit. And try to do better.

Being accountable to yourself can be difficult. Don't rely on memory. I've tried that method myself. It was really hard—and largely unsuccessful.

VULNERABILITY

Vulnerability is the sister to accountability. Being open to growth doesn't come easy for most of us, but it's almost always easier than not doing it.

A lot has been written about vulnerability. Brené Brown's work is particularly revealing. I urge you to check it out. I won't detail it here, but it's worth looking into as it can help open your eyes to what vulnerability looks like and how to benefit from it.

When you let your hair down and really expose yourself to feedback and self-discovery, you can make great gains in your leadership growth. Resisting feedback or being unwilling to seek it at all can quickly hamper your growth. Have you ever used the words "that wasn't as bad as I thought it would be?" I have. Resistance prevents you from learning, which prevents you from growing. Being vulnerable opens those doors.

Here are some techniques and benefits to being open to new ideas and feedback:

- **Ask for feedback:** This is the classic technique. Just ask what others think. Then listen.

- **Listen to the feedback:** This is the hard part for most of us. You've asked. Now listen (yes, I said it again—it's that hard).

- **Ask for more:** Sensing a theme? When you hear something difficult, rather than defend your position, try this: "That's good to know. Can you tell me more?"

- **Relationships will improve:** In time, the more you do this, the more people will open up to you. You'll get better information and they'll want to help you. Relationships actually improve when people feel you trust them. They might return the favor by asking for help themselves.

- **You will improve:** Once you've gotten past the disappointment and just marinate in the feedback (you're a spare rib soaking up the goodness here), you'll usually find things you can benefit from.

Vulnerability gets easier with time. It doesn't come easy at first for most of us, but it will get better. And the benefits you'll receive make it worth it. Stick with it. You'll be glad you did.

PERCEPTION

This is one of my favorite topics to speak to.

Perception is all about how you see the world.

Your own senses and beliefs shape your view of the world and your leadership. The difficulty in this is that your own feelings about your leadership abilities may not match what others think.

This doesn't have to be all bad news. Sometimes, you're hard on yourself and don't feel as good about your talents as others do. It can be welcome news to find out you're doing better than you thought. On the other hand, when you believe you're doing well and others don't share that view, it can be deflating and hard to accept.

Perception is an important concept to understand. It's also important and gratifying to know that you can control it. You have the power to help others see your talents. You control your actions and your beliefs. When you shape them appropriately, your audience will believe you and follow you.

This is tied very closely to accountability and vulnerability. Taken together, these concepts can really help you improve. Here are tips as to how to factor perception into your development:

- **Ask for feedback:** This is similar to the task in vulnerability but with a twist. Ask for feedback and then compare it to your own belief. As an example, ask how well you communicate. How does it match up with your beliefs?

- **Ask for advice:** If you receive feedback that doesn't match with your own belief, ask what would make the other person feel differently. Use this type of question: "How could I communicate with you in a way that would feel more effective to you?" Shape your actions in a way that matches the needs of others.

- **Look in the mirror:** When you lack access to others, practice "looking in the mirror." How do you believe others would see you? Don't just ask how you see yourself. Put yourself in their shoes. Do this for successes and failures. Why were you successful or why did you fail? This is particularly helpful when you got an outcome you didn't expect.

Getting a reality check on your perceptions is a critical concept. It can really help with blind spots. Knowing how you're seen by those you work with can help you shape how you want to be seen. It's difficult at times, but it's time well worth spending.

GROUP DEVELOPMENT

While individual development can be effective, group work has some real advantages. There are times when it's just too hard to be that honest with yourself or when you just can't see what someone else is seeing.

Group development isn't simply asking for feedback. The difference is that you work as a team so that all the members learn and grow together. Just asking others for feedback is an individual approach—you're just gathering data for personal reflection. In a "learning group," you all commit to providing feedback and insight to one another so everyone improves.

Learning groups have another advantage. You get to know everyone's strengths and weaknesses. In this way, you can find natural mentoring connections in which you can teach and support one another. Remember to "cross pollinate." Look for people who are stronger at areas you want to work on while lining yourself up with peers who need support doing what you do best.

It isn't critical if everyone knows about the Square and the Triangle, but it helps if you can all speak the same language. Share what you know or encourage them to get a copy of the book. When you all speak the same leadership language, you can better support each other's growth without having to decode what you all mean.

If your organization doesn't have learning groups, you can form your own. Start small. Even one other person helps, or maybe two or three. Look for peers who have a like-minded interest in growing and for people who will be candid enough to provide feedback.

Take your time developing as a team. If you haven't done this before, building some trust early helps as you get to digging deeper into your collective growth. Set some ground rules and follow them. As an example, discuss how feedback should be delivered or how to politely redirect unwanted or unhelpful behavior. Be forgiving of each other and respect that it takes time to learn how to be candid with one another. Done well and done patiently, you'll get rewarded in a way you'll find difficult to emulate on your own.

JOY

Personal growth is difficult. Or at least it's portrayed that way.

If I've learned anything over my career, it was that too much time was spent focusing on the negative in leadership development circles. There was too much focus on leaders' weak areas and too much negative talk about the difficulty and pain we experience when we grow.

Two very different experiences have caused me to realize that we're missing the fun in leading.

I had some difficult experiences during my time in healthcare that rocked me for a while. A bad patient outcome (an accidental death) coupled with having to remove some executives whom I considered friends resulted in a lot of change in my world. New leaders came on board and my world was upside down in an instant. Suffice it to say, I experienced emotions I hope never to repeat and I had to dig deep in the well to find my way out.

Fortunately, I found it within me to seek the help of a coach who helped me claw my way back out. I owe her a lot. I also owe my wife a lot. Between the two of them, I rediscovered what I love about my work. It came in the initial guise of improving my leadership connection, but it was ultimately about rediscovering joy. It was one of the hardest lessons of my career, but I survived it and I ended up in a better place because of it. In retrospect, the situation was just a trigger for a storm that had probably been already brewing. I hope never to repeat it but I'm grateful for it, nonetheless.

On a lighter note, I was a fly-fishing guide earlier in my life and a fly-tying instructor. People came to me to learn how to make a fly rod work and tie flies. These students knew little about the sport; sometimes they knew nothing at all. They were forced to demonstrate vulnerability and accountability constantly. They had to demonstrate what I taught them, which could be scary and embarrassing for them as most of them doubted their talent.

Yet these students were always excited to learn. They didn't really suffer from having to be on stage or being at varying levels of learning with each other. Why? Because they loved what they were learning. Making a fly rod work or tying flies was worth pursuing. And so was the path to get there.

If you actually love to lead, then getting better at it won't feel like work. You certainly won't dread it when it's difficult. Let your joy of doing what you love feed your desire to get better. Leading people and getting things done can be fun.

If you wrap up accountability, vulnerability, and perception in a blanket of joy, I promise you'll grow faster with fewer bumps and bruises than if you force yourself to get better at something you don't like anyway.

Find the joy in your work and your growth, and you'll be rewarded in ways you can't imagine.

DEVELOPMENT PLAN AND CASE STUDY

Developing your leadership style and abilities requires a plan. While it would be hard for me to recommend specific details for your plan without sitting down with you, let me give you a general formula to consider. I also want to present a short "case study" of a leader I worked with at recent company. The case study demonstrates how to start putting the Square and Triangle to work for you.

Development Plan

1. Review chapter 9—Strengthen Your Square or Triangle.

    a. Ensure you're building accountability, vulnerability, perception, and joy into your plan.

    b. Where possible, involve feedback partners.

2. Assess whether you are rooted in the Square or the Triangle.

3. Review chapter 4 – The Square and the Triangle.

    a. Create a drawing that represents your foundational structure—get to know it. I mean *really* know it.

4. Review chapters 6, 7, and 8 closely. Pay attention to those elements that tie to your foundation, but don't forget the other—you need both the Square and the Triangle to succeed.

5. As you come to understand what is natural and unnatural for you, identify strategies you can adopt in the work you do to improve. Focus on leveraging and integrating your foundation into your plan.

Case Study

Mason (not his real name) was a leader who developed his skills and became more comfortable in his leadership role through the Square and the Triangle.

Like many managers, Mason had difficulty managing difficult employees. He dreaded giving feedback and managing performance. He wanted his team to like him and hoped that kindness and his skill with team dynamics would help his underperformers get better. Sadly, neither were working for him.

He met with me, as a mentor, and I shared the Square and Triangle with him. After some initial interviewing, we learned that keeping relationships steady and keeping the team harmonious were priorities to him. He also shared that getting his team to adopt new strategies and implement new procedures was difficult. He quickly saw that his foundation was in the Square.

After further review, it was apparent that his team really liked him. He was a good "people" person. However, he wasn't getting the most from his team. He was afraid to stress the relationships.

As we worked together, he began to discover that by failing to address individual issues, especially with underperformers, his good staff members were getting disgruntled. The "cancerous" employees were making it hard on everyone. In short, Mason learned that by ignoring one person, he was in fact hurting the whole team. He also learned that his team supported him taking action. Mason came to realize that managing "people" problems didn't frighten his team, it engaged them. The team knew he cared about them when he addressed difficult situations.

Mason improved by more purposefully utilizing his strength in managing relationships to help him get results. We created nurturing but firm conversations that protected the dignity of the difficult employee but made it clear things had to improve. The team, indirectly, became braver in helping their peer improve—they too wanted to help but wouldn't accept their peer's negativity anymore. The team literally helped Mason manage the issue as their trust in him improved.

Mason learned that by leaning into his Square with purpose and intent, he could improve results and performance. He ultimately got more confident in directing the work to be done while using the trust he'd built with his team to his advantage.

Mason was ultimately able to make these improvements because he was accountable and vulnerable. He opened himself up to feedback. He found that he enjoyed leading when he believed he could do it better. He also found that focusing on a small drawing of a Square under a Triangle was all he needed to be reminded of how to integrate relationships and results into the culture of his department.

TAKE-HOME MESSAGES

△ Being accountable to yourself and vulnerable to others promotes growth.

△ Perception and self-awareness make growth easier to see.

△ Bring joy to your development—learning should be fun.

FINAL THOUGHTS

Freedom

Congratulations! You've just taken your first steps toward simplifying your leadership life. It's quite possible that you already have a lot of leadership books on your shelf. All of them seemed good at the time you bought them; they held some nugget that either served you well or at least got you to thinking. You might also have a hard drive full of leadership tools and reports that describe your behavior and traits in great detail. Can you remember any of it? Do you use it or reflect upon it?

USE THIS BOOK

Reading this book is an important shift for you. Rather than just adding this book to your collection, you're now perfectly positioned to put the Square and the Triangle to work for you. Don't let this book collect dust. I urge you to dog-ear it, highlight it, and keep it close to you while you put the principles between its covers to work for you. Use it when you need a refresher. Then, get your markers or your pencils and draw squares and triangles for yourself. What do you see in the pictures that can help you improve your leadership?

SIMPLIFY

Leadership development should be easy. Take this book and go look at your leadership life through the lens of simplicity. Simplify what you see—how can you better influence others and get things accomplished? When you take this refreshed and clearer approach to your work, you'll be more successful, more easily. Leading others should be noble and enriching work. When you take this simplified approach, you'll benefit from the joy leadership brings and the freedom to focus on what's important.

VISION

Have a vision for what successful leadership will look like and what your Square and Triangle look like. Are you leaning toward the "people" side of your leadership picture? How can you take advantage of that natural ability? Are you the results guru? How can you use that talent to ensure you lead through others? Draw your own pictures, study them, and see what they tell you.

PRACTICE

Practice! Don't just assume reading the book is all you need. Learning happens most when we practice. Books account for as little as 10 percent of overall learning, according to some studies. Jay Cross, in his "Informal Learning Blog" and book *Informal Learning: Rediscovering the Natural Pathways That Inspire Innovation and Performance*, has compiled a lot of research that demonstrates this and how important informal learning (practice) is when compared to formal learning like books and workshops. Pierre Gurdjian, et al., of McKinsey & Company, describes how leadership development fails at times because organizations don't tie practice to the work being performed.

Practicing what you read is how you remember what you read. Practicing in the context of your work makes it more real. Practicing helps you develop the strength of habit you can rely on. Use this book as your personal coach while you practice!

The Square and the Triangle offer you a freedom from the complexity of leadership. They offer you an easy-to-remember and easy-to-follow path to improve, thrive, and love being a leader. Live by the lessons they teach you. They are your constant companions as you grow your leadership.

Love being a leader. Let me say that again. Can you imagine loving your leadership role? I think you can. As you become increasingly effective and proactive, you will love being a leader. Share your stories and bring some friends along with you on your journey toward less conflict and more victories in your day. Better leadership is right around the corner.

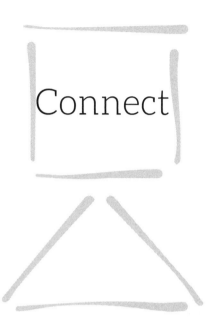

Connect

Thanks for taking the time to share in something that I am so passionate about seeing brought to life in your own leadership. Your participation in this style of leadership means the world to me. Send me an email to mark@ thesquareandthetriangle. com or comment on social media so we can engage in this important dialogue. Find me by googling "The Square and the Triangle" or go directly to TheSquareandtheTriangle.com.

Resources

CHAPTER NOTES

Chapter 1 – Why Simplicity?

Merriam-Webster Online, s.v. "Occam's razor," accessed August 17, 2017, https://www.merriam-webster.com/dictionary/Occam's%20razor.

Gibbs, Phil, and Sugihara Hiroshi. "The Original Usenet Physics FAQ," *What Is Occam's Razor?* UC Riverside, July 2017. www.math.ucr.edu/home/baez/physics/General/occam.html

Encyclopædia Britannica Online, Vignaux, Paul D., s.v. "William of Ockham," accessed August 17, 2017, www.britannica.com/biography/William-of-Ockham.

Carlson, Ben. "Why Simple Beats Complex." *A Wealth of Common Sense*. Cafemedia, July 9, 2017. http://awealthofcommonsense.com/2017/07/why-simple-beats-complex/

Chapter 3 – Balance

Merriam-Webster Online, s.v. "balance," accessed August 17, 2017, https://www.merriam-webster.com/dictionary/balance.

Final Thoughts – Freedom

Cross, Jay. "Where Did the 80% Come from?" *Informal Learning Blog RSS*, Internet Time Alliance, 2007, www.informl.com/where-did-the-80-come-from/

Cross, Jay. *Informal Learning: Rediscovering the Natural Pathways That Inspire Innovation and Performance.* Wiley, 2011.

Gurdjian, Pierre, Thomas Halbeisen, and Kevin Lane. "Why Leadership-Development Programs Fail." McKinsey & Company, January 2014. www.mckinsey.com/global-themes/leadership/why-leadership-development-programs-fail.

RECOMMENDED READING

Allen, David. *Getting Things Done: The Art of Stress-Free Productivity*, revised edition. New York: Penguin Books, 2015.

Brown, Brené. *Daring Greatly: How the Courage to Be Vulnerable Transforms the Way We Live, Love, Parent, and Lead*. New York: Avery, 2012.

Christensen, Clayton, et al. *On Managing Yourself*. Brighton: Harvard Business School Publishing Corporation, 2010.

Cross, Jay. *Informal Learning: Rediscovering the Natural Pathways That Inspire Innovation and Performance*. San Francisco: Pfeiffer, 2006.

George, Bill. *Discover Your True North*, 2nd edition. San Francisco: Jossey-Bass, 2015.

Goleman, Daniel. *Leadership That Gets Results (Harvard Business Classics)*. Brighton: Harvard Business School Publishing Corporation, 2017.

Grenny, Joseph, et al. *Influencer: The New Science of Leading Change*, 2nd edition. New York: McGraw-Hill Education, 2013.

Hanh, Thich Nhat. *Work: How to Find Joy and Meaning in Each Hour of the Day*. Berkley: Parallax Press, 2008.

Hughes, Terri. *Simple Shifts: Effective Leadership Changes Everything*. Eagle: Aloha Publishing, 2014.

Kaye, Beverly & Jordan-Evans, Sharon. *Love 'Em or Lose 'Em: Getting Good People to Stay*, 5th edition. Oakland: Berrett-Koehler Publishers, 2014.

Lama, Dalai & Tutu, Desmond. *The Book of Joy: Lasting Happiness in a Changing World.* New York: Avery, 2016.

Lencioni, Patrick. *The Five Dysfunctions of a Team: A Leadership Fable.* San Francisco: Jossey-Bass, 2002.

Acknowledgments

I learned a lot about relationships and results in writing this book, and I have a new-found respect for the phrase "it takes a village."

I want to begin by thanking Terri Hughes, Executive Leadership Coach and author of *Simple Shifts* (also available from Aloha Publishing). Terri saw me through some hard moments in my career. I'm a better person and leader for it. Her work also helped me find Aloha Publishing.

Certainly, I must thank my new friends and colleagues at Aloha. Jen Regner, the lead editor, taught me a lot about polishing rocks into gems. Thank you for your many hours of making this book become what it was supposed to be. I'm beyond grateful. Thank you to Melissa Lambert. In addition to marketing support, Melissa helped me shape my purpose as a consultant. She also laughed at my jokes. The check is in the mail.

A very profound thank you to Maryanna Young. From my initial 15-minute cold call and subsequent three-hour business meeting to pitch her this book idea, through the many hours of discussions about Squares and Triangles, Maryanna has believed in this project and in me. Talk about building confidence! Thank you for making this project so much better than I could have imagined.

To Sean Lynch: Sean is an impressive leader and a childhood friend. As my martial arts companion, he more than anyone will know about cannons and bamboo platforms. We've fished together, written together, played lots of chess, and clearly determined the direction the world should take. We've opted to keep it secret because of our mutual love of suspense. He provided me with fabulous feedback on this book that took it from so-so to great. Thank you, my friend!

To my mother, Barbara. Despite her own personal reservations, she provided me with very helpful feedback, which helped shape this work.

To my stepchildren, Bryli and Breah. They are patiently awaiting the book I promised them, *Life With Girls*. In the meantime, they've taught me a thing or two about relationships, results, and love regardless of who you are or where you come from. They make me feel right at home.

And most certainly, thank you to Shelly, my wife. She has endured much in the making of this book, including my sudden career change to author, consultant, and mentor, and her sudden career addition: becoming my sounding board throughout this process. She knows a lot about *The Square and the Triangle*. This book wouldn't have happened without her. I thank her for helping me find my way through this project and life. She provided me with many opportunities to put this into practice, at work and at home. Husbands should be so lucky. Turns out I am. I love you, darling.

Lastly, to the leaders over the last 10 years who have experienced the Square and the Triangle. I appreciate your help in shaping this work. It wouldn't exist without you. Many thanks! Now, go tell your friends!

About the Author

Mark Stevens is the owner of The Square and the Triangle, Coaching and HR Consulting, Inc. He is a highly skilled human resources professional, having served in senior level roles in healthcare, biomedical/pharmaceutical, logistics, and retail. His experience is extensive, including all facets of human resources—employee and labor relations, recruitment and talent acquisition, talent management, and leadership development. He has provided HR support in multiple states including Idaho, Utah, Montana, Colorado, and California.

Mark is especially passionate about leadership development and has developed and taught "The Square and the Triangle" concepts to many leaders for 10 years. His focus on simplicity has helped these leaders achieve success quickly and easily. Mark helps leaders spend more time leading and learning by removing the weight of more complicated concepts that inevitably get dropped rather than put into practice.

He is a gifted and entertaining public speaker. He loves to bring his passion and humor to his audiences. Attendees to his seminars and classes routinely describe how much they learn and how enjoyable his speaking style is.

Mark Stevens calls Twin Falls, Idaho, home. He is happily married to his wife, Shelly, and together, they enjoy raising her three children and loving on two cats and a dog. Mark loves spending time in the outdoors with his family. He and Shelly are avid cyclists and ride the roads and trails near their home. Mark was also a fly-fishing guide and loves to spend time in the rivers throughout the Mountain West.